The Doctrines of Grace

GEORGE S. BISHOP

BAKER BOOK HOUSE
Grand Rapids, Michigan

Paperback edition issued 1977
by Baker Book House Company
ISBN: 0-8010-0715-1

PHOTOLITHOPRINTED BY CUSHING - MALLOY, INC.
ANN ARBOR, MICHIGAN, UNITED STATES OF AMERICA
1977

CONTENTS

		Page
	Preface	3
1	The Ultimate Appeal	7
2	The Testimony of the Scripture to Itself	19
3	Inspiration of the Hebrew Vowel-Points	43
4	The Principles of Revision	60
5	Relative Value of the Old Testament	88
6	Cosmogony in Genesis	101
7	Jonah—The Keystone of the Testaments	119
8	Difficulties in the Bible	131
9	The Bondage of the Will	144
10	The Doctrine of Grace	153
11	The Doctrine of Election True	167
12	A Popular Talk on Election	179

PREFACE

It is by many assumed and indeed most confidently asserted that the Doctrines of Grace; as preached by Augustine, Anselm, Calvin and the great Reformers—have had their day—are superseded by the breadth of modern thought—are held, in their original integrity, by no one now; nor can they now be put, as they were put four hundred years ago, with hope of conviction or chance of success.

It is in honest and earnest dissent from such an opinion—an opinion sufficiently confuted by the marvelous power and success of men like Charles H. Spurgeon, Caesar Malan, Robert Murray McCheyne and the great leaders of the Scottish Free Church Disruption—that the following discourses are republished, as they and others have been delivered during a ministry of more than forty years, to the edification of thousands and the conversion of scores and hundreds of souls.

There are but two religions on earth. One based upon the postulate of Free Will; the other upon that of Free Grace. The two mutually annihilate and replace one another. For, if a man is saved in any way, either in whole or in part, by the exercise of his own will, he is not saved *only* by God's will; and if he is saved only by God's will—i. e., of pure grace, he is not saved by his own. Divine Election, therefore, underlies religion as it underlies Revelation. "It is," says Toplady, "the golden thread which runs through the whole Christian System. For, what Cicero asserts of human learning—when he says; *Omnes artes quae ad humanitatem pertinent, habent quoddam commune vinculum, et quasi cognatione quadam inter se continentur.* The whole circle of the arts has a kind of mutual bond and connection, and by a certain reciprocal relationship are they held and interwoven together—can be more exactly asserted of Divine Election. It is the one bond which unites and keeps together the entire Christian System; without which, it were a system of sand ever falling to fragments."

If our race possesses a free will to do that which is good, then faith is an act of my own and from me, and I may relinquish or lose it. There is thus no certain salvation. If, on the other hand; Man fallen can do nothing but fall and cannot will upward; then, God must interpose to give him that will in the counter-direction. But, then, in that case, he is saved by God's will and not by his own. And that is Election.

In other words: God must begin. His must be the first impulse and movement. What are all the after influences of God, no matter how potent, if it remains with the man to put himself, or not, under those influences? Does not the man, and not God, in that case, decide his salvation? Is he not, in fact his own Saviour? If man begins, contradicting St. Paul, he "makes himself to differ" and is, in fact the author of the "new creature." In other words, he becomes his own God and his Free Will is set up like Dagon over against the Ark and is, henceforth his Idol. For to be the author of the new creation is a greater thing than to be Author of the old. There is therefore no *anknüpfungspunkt*—no point of contact between free will and free grace. They are diametrical opposites. The Scripture says that men are dead in sin. Can a dead man will anything? Can a corpse decide its own destiny? In one way, it can. It can work out its own dissolution. The other way, it cannot. It can destroy but not save itself: it cannot give itself the vital spark: "Salvation is of the Lord." The religion of free grace therefore gives the lie to that of free will. The only freedom possible to fallen man is freedom *to sin* and freedom *from holiness*.

"But why insist on a point which is, after all, an abstraction?" Simply because it is not an abstraction; for the man who trusts his free will is a *lost* man whatever may be his attainments in virtue. His Pharisaism: his contending the point of precedence with God: his obstinate holding to his own ability, will damn him. God is determined to save by free grace; the man is determined to save himself by free will. He is trying to stem Niagara by swimming. Without rescue from outside he will be swept down.

This is the great controversy which is abroad in the world and which decides *destiny,* as it divides mankind. Does God save me, or do I, by the use of grace common to all, save myself? Does God have all the glory—the undivided glory; does He by a Sovereign Election and choice make me, from *unwilling*, willing? Or do I elect my own self and initiate salvation, and will because I have power? And do I still contend it that men can come to Christ without the "drawing of the Father:" that from unwilling they can make themselves willing without any "day of God's power:" that it *is* of him that willeth and of him that runneth whether or not God sheweth mercy, and that the carnal mind is subject to the law of God and indeed can be, so then they that are in the flesh *can* by trying hard, please Him!

This is the great controversy which man has with God— a controversy in which man must be put down and his ability to will annihilated and he lie dead in full surrender at the footstool of a Sovereignty which hath mercy on whom it will have mercy; or he must continue to stand up and brave God and fight to the last for the power of his self-reversible will and go down to hell a lost man.

The defence of the Doctrines of Grace is therefore a defence of religion. Should these doctrines cease to be preached, religion would become a shipwreck and the Church an apostasy. The reason of the present ominous and alarming declension in opinions and morals—the reason why the Church cannot get the ear of the world; why she has no practical power to transform, is because she has no supernatural voice—no *"Thus saith the Lord!"*—no deep and tremendous conviction. Ethics can be preached without the Holy Ghost. So can any system of Moral Reform whatsoever; but Regeneration—the doctrine which lays man stark helpless before God—shut up to a faith which is the gift of mere Sovereign distinguishing grace—is a doctrine which calls for the Spirit of God who alone can breathe true conviction; who alone can quicken the dead and say to countless dry bones which lie bleaching at the mouth of the Sepulchre—*"Live!"* in the cyclone and sweep of a mighty revival. As well preach to the mummies of Egypt as preach to unconverted souls without the Holy Ghost.

The Sovereignty of God in Salvation! This is the πρῶτον θεμέλιον the Ground and Base of the Gospel. How shall we lift the masses if this fulcrum be removed? How shall the doctrine, either, prove its potency without that all prevailing prayer which "thunders in the ears of God and brings down copious blessings from on high?"

The return to Calvinism is a return to first principles and to "first love." It is the slinging again of the *five* smooth stones from the brook which brings down proud Goliath, the mighty self-inflated giant of free thought, in the presence of the weak-kneed armies of Israel. It is the multiplication, by the power of God's Spirit of *five* poor barley loaves which means the feeding again and again of hungry five thousands. It is the echo of that trumpet of the Holy War whose no uncertain Summons calls "the sacramental host of God's elect" from lethargy to life; from victory to victory; from conquering to conquer.

If the Lord shall deign, in any least degree to own and bless again the paragraphs which follow; ours shall be the *mercy, HIS ALONE THE PRAISE.*

THE ULTIMATE APPEAL

Isa. viii:20

"To the law and to the testimony: if they speak not according to this Word, it is because there is no light in them."

Religion, from *re-ligo* "to bind back," must have something to tie to. It must have a foundation, a basis, an ultimate appeal. What is that appeal?

Some say, to *consciousness;* man finds God by consulting himself; what tallies with himself is Divine. God is humanity colossalized. This is the religion of nature. It will account for every vagary, from the myths of Paganism to the self delusions of Theosophy and Christian Science—for everything from Homer to Huxley.

Some say the appeal is to *tradition;* to the decree of Councils; to the Fathers; to an authority lodged in the Church as a Divine corporation breathed in, guided, made infallible by the presence of the Holy Ghost. This is the doctrine of Rome—a doctrine which binds to a system assumed to be supernatural, but shifting as the decrees of councils have shifted; contradictory as the statements of church fathers are conflicting; blind and confusing; a congeries of truths and errors; of affirmations and denials; of half lights and evasions, from Origen to Bellarmime.

The third appeal is to a *Book* in its two Testaments, from cover to cover, Infallible; without contradiction, without confusion and without mistake; in every chapter, verse and letter inspired, imperative, direct, divine. The Bible is the basis, measure, criterion and test of true religion. That which binds back to God is the Word which came from God; a Revelation and authority which speaks from heaven compelling the conscience and subjugating the will. "*Thus saith the Lord!*" is our apology and our appeal when, as ministers of Christ and prophets bearing the credentials of His high commission, we address ourselves to men. "To the law and to the testimony: if they speak not according to this Word, it is because there is no light in them." The Bible like the world stands upon nothing. It is its own self-evidence—its own imperial assertion. It is the voice of

God which waits for no defence; for no endorsement, but which claims submission. To receive it is salvation—to reject it, trifle with it, question it is to make shipwreck of the soul.

The Bible is a direct Revelation from God—a voice speaking from heaven. How is that evident?

1. From its *uniqueness*: the Bible differs on its surface from every other book.

It speaks a Trinity in the very roots of its verbs, every one of which is, in the Hebrew, composed of 3 letters—tri-literal.

It teaches man's apostasy and restoration in the singular reversal of its text. The Hebrew is written and read from right to left; from God's right hand where He doth work, is man's departure. Then the Greek takes him up, a prodigal son at his remotest distance from God and brings him back from left to right—from death to life again.

Incarnation is in the Tetragrammation; that is the Hebrew letters of the word Jehovah יְהֹוָה written vertically from up to down give us the outlines of the human figure—God made flesh. This is the difference between Elohim, God in creation; and God in covenant anticipating incarnation.

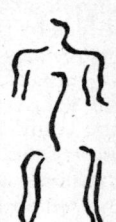

Again: the Bible puts man's true relations in the very conjugation of the Hebrew verb. In all occidental languages the verb is conjugated from the first person to the third—"I," "Thou," "He." The Hebrew, in reversal of the human thought, is conjugated from the third down and back to the first: beginning with God, then my neighbor, then myself last—"He," "Thou," "I." This is the Divine order self obliterating and beautiful.

Again: The Bible is divine in its perfect self-consistency, —in the comparison and harmony of spiritual things with spiritual. *Ponderibus librata suis*: everywhere it is equally balanced in its teachings and its mighty words.

THE DOCTRINES OF GRACE 9

Again: The Bible is divine in its illimitable Comprehensiveness. The Hebrew language has no present tense. The present moment is but a vanishing point. The Bible lives in an Eternal NOW. Infinitely above man, the Bible is let down to man who is "but of yesterday and knows nothing."

The Bible is divine in its Arithmetic. Everything in the universe is built on numbers. We say, "Figures will not lie." Numbers are in the Bible and everywhere each bears the same significance and indicates the same relationship. Numbers are in the Bible. Criticism is confronted by the fact. Does criticism dare deny that God is in the fact? Does criticism dare assert that there is not, at work in the Scripture, the grandest Mathematician of all—God ciphering out the problem of destiny? Take some of these numbers. 3, which always stands for Trinity and *trinal relation*. 4, which designates *human nature* in its possibilities and weakness—the four corners of the habitable globe. 5, *responsibility* to God as seen in the five senses—the five fingers of the right hand. So Israel went up out of Egypt, "five in a rank." So the height of the hangings of the Tabernacle *looking upward* was five cubits. Take further: 6, always *one short of perfection*. 7, the *Mediator's number* 3 and 4 united—*God and man*, Redemption complete. 8, a new octave—*resurrection*. 10, a double five—ten fingers on two hands—ten commandments, *responsibility to God and man*. 40, *trial, probation*—forty years of Moses in the wilderness—forty days on Sinai—forty days of temptation for our Lord. These meanings are unchangeable. Let him who denies it, try to change them and make them anything else if he can. To do so he must change the 6 fingers and 6 toes of Goliath, the 6 pieces of his armor, the 600 shekels weight of his spear's head, the 6 cubits of his stature which lay prostrate under David's sling and stone. To disprove the meaning of the 6, the critic must deny the 66 cubits in the height of Nebuchadnezzar's image and the 6 cubits of its breadth as it goes down before the smiting Stone. To disprove the meaning of the 6, the critic must go on to deny 666 to be the number of that Antichrist, typed by Goliath and by Nebuchadnezzar, who falls before a greater David and a greater unhewn Stone—"Whom the Lord shall consume with the spirit of his mouth and destroy with the brightness of His coming." Let the critic stand in front of the black-board which displays these figures, and laugh at their absurdity if he can. If he cannot laugh, let him be silent and wonder and adore.

The Bible differs from every other book in the Perpetuity of its text—that it is written in the only two languages which—dating back of all tradition are recognized as living vehicles of thought to-day. The Greek spoken in the streets of modern Athens is the same Greek to its very accents as is that of Xenophon, and of the Iliad which was penned three thousand years ago. The Hebrew of the Talmud is the Hebrew of Genesis. Marvellous survival, and miracle of God! The Egyptian of Rameses has perished. The Assyrian spoken by Rabshakeh is gone but the Greek spoken by St. Paul on Areopagus finds echo still beneath the Arch of Hadrian and the sacred languages in which God wrote, like the cloven tongues of Pentecost flash still a living fire while their archaic characters, unworn and undecayed by time, lie moveless and immutable at the foundation of all that can pretend to solid learning or a liberal culture. Without them, Theological Seminaries and Colleges as well, are without the guarantee or hope of either prosperity or influence or permanence.

The Bible is the one Book in the world which can be read only in the light of supernatural illumination.* In *this*, it stands unique, exclusive, singular, isolate. Other books, Plato, Shakespeare, Bacon, Descartes, can be understood as well by the natural man as by the spiritual,—but no natural man can know the things of the Bible but by the Holy Ghost who wrote the Bible. The natural man, even the wisest, the most learned of natural men, sticks in the letter. He gets no further than the text. The most illiterate peasant taught by the Spirit sees more of God in His Word than does the greatest philosopher, or the profoundest technical theologian who is without that teaching. The Bible is a light which requires an additional Light. "In Thy light shall we see light." "Open Thou mine eyes that I may behold wondrous things out of Thy law." "Then opened He their understanding that they might un-

---

*"No man sees one iota in the Scripture," says Luther, "but he that hath the Spirit of God."

derstand the Scriptures." A man may have the Bible and read it through 10,000 times and the letter may kill him. Unitarians have the Bible but they cannot see Christ in it. "For what man can know the things of a man if he has not a man's spirit in him? Even so, the things of God cannot any man know if he has not God's spirit in him" (1 Cor. ii:2). Regeneration determines theology.

The Bible is unique, apart from every other book in its *Self-evidence*. When the sun shines you do not fly to a laborious argument to prove there is a sun; or that sunlight is irradiation. The sun speaks for himself. He simply says, "I am the sun." He needs not to say it, he shines it.

So the Word of God. The Koran does not on the face of it say, "I am divine!" It does not glow with God from its pages. So neither does the Zenda-Vesta or the Book of Mormon.

But the Bible *shines what it is*. It asks no apology; its voice is its claim. We take the ground that when one hears the Bible he knows by instinct that it is the Word of God—he recognizes its celestial tone.

We take the open ground that a single stray leaf of God's Word found by the wayside, by one who never had seen it before, would convince him at once that the strange and wonderful words were those of his God—were Divine.

The Scriptures are their own self-evidence. We take the ground the sun requires no critic—truth no diving-bell. When the sun shines, he *shines* the sun. When God speaks, His evidence is in the accents of His words.

How did the prophets of old know, when God spoke to them that it was God? Did they subject the voice that shook their every bone and made their flesh dissolve upon them, to a critical test? Did they put God, so to say—as some of our moderns seem to have done—into a crucible, into a chemist's retort, in order to certify that He was God? Did they find it necessary to hold the handwriting of God in front of the blowpipe of anxious philosophical examination in order to bring out and to make the invisible, visible? The very suggestion is madness. Inability to comprehend the words of God does not arise from their obscurity and our weakness, but from our wicked aversion to things most plainly uttered. "The light shineth in darkness and the darkness does not even know that it is light."

The Bible is a Divine Revelation. It is to be handled with awe. It is to be received on the knees of the soul.

2. *The Bible speaks with authority.* It *claims* to be Divine. It is not man's utterance. It is everywhere, "Thus saith the Lord!" Twenty six times in the 27 chapters of Leviticus, the formula is repeated: "And the Lord spake unto Moses saying." Moses then was but the recorder of what the Lord said.

Evolution says the world came out of a fire mist. Genesis tells us that the heavens and the earth were an instant creation—that God spake and it was done; that He commanded and it stood fast. 35 times the word *God* appears in the 34 verses which complete the account of creation and end with the Sabbath. God created the *heavens* and the *earth;* God created great *whales;* God created *man* in the image of God; God created *the seed* before it sprouted in the earth, etc., etc. These 35 repetitions—these 35 assertions of God are 35 red hot cannon balls between the eyes of evolution. Before them, like Goliath, it falls to the ground.

The Bible speaks with authority—

"This is the Judge that ends the strife,
Where wit and wisdom fail."

The Bible is unique—the Bible speaks with authority—then

3. *The Bible meets the soul's supremest need.* It does this because it deals with 3 infinites,—infinite holiness; infinite guilt; infinite atonement.

Infinite holiness. God is holy—utterly and absolutely holy. But, if holy, God is just, for justice is a part of holiness. But, if just He is of purer eyes than to behold iniquity. When I look up to God I see infinite holiness— whiteness which penetrates my black soul with horror.

For I am guilty. I feel it, and the more I look down into myself, the more do I feel it. I find that I am not only a sinner, but sinful—that it is in me to sin and that the tendency downward is a fact irreversible; depravity is a pit that is bottomless. That is the second infinite—infinite guilt.

Here then are two infinites directly opposed. Up there, God. Down here, my soul. How can they be reconciled? The never to be stifled cry of the awakened spirit is: "How can God be just and justify the guilty?"

The Bible and the Bible alone answers that question. It brings in the third infinite. One as near to me in my nature as he is to God in the Divine, has come in between us. "See God our Shield!" A screen is interposed between the infinites, as infinite as they. The question of my aching heart, which all the universe outside it, could not answer, the Bible answers when it whispers, "He is our Peace."

> But when Immanuel's face appears,
>   My thoughts no comfort find;
> The holy, just and sacred Three,
>   Are terrors to my mind.
>
> But when Immanuel's face appears,
>   My joys, my hopes begin;
> His *name* forbids my slavish fears,
>   His *grace* removes my sin.

4. As the Bible meets the soul's supremest need, so it reveals a *method of salvation* which man could never have imagined and which shown to him, he cannot consent to receive.

For the Bible teaches that we are justified by another man's merits—in other words that we can have no merits of our own but must consent to be accepted only on the ground of what Jesus the Son of God has suffered and done.

Not another book in the world has ever taught or suggested such a notion as this. Last winter, in Egypt, I read a treatise written in the time of Rameses II, by Ptah-Hotep, one of his Counsellors of State. It went to show how a man can be right with God. He must make *himself* right. He must be just, true, virtuous, temperate. In other words, the book written by an old Egyptian 4,000 years ago taught salvation by ethics. That is what Socrates taught, what Zoroaster taught and Confucius. That is the doctrine of the world and even where Christ is accepted the doctrine is still: "We must do something; we must do our part; we must trust Christ and *do the best we can,* then God will accept us."

The Church of Rome teaches that Christ by His sufferings merited a grace for us, by using which, *we may merit* and so be accepted for what we have done. This doctrine of being saved either in whole or in part by our doings is the doctrine of every unregenerate man whether so-called Christian or Pagan.

The Bible shows itself Divine by showing a Diviner way. It shoves man from the platform and replaces him by a Substitute—what the law could not do in that it was weak through the flesh, Christ has done and done wholly. Adam lies dead and we in him lie dead in trespasses and sins—Christ stands on resurrection ground—and faith, a single, simple, solitary act of faith—by one bound transports us to His side.

Adam disobeyed the law; we disobey it. God insists that we shall keep it perfectly. He cannot insist upon anything less. We cannot keep it perfectly. Then Christ does it for us.

Christ for 33 years—the period of a human lifetime, was, under the law, keeping the law to make for us a record. He earned heaven for us on the principle, "Do this and live"—Christ *did* and we plead His merit.

I get heaven simply on the ground of Christ's performances.—His righteous life. His obedience reckoned mine, is my obedience.

But—that righteousness of Christ for me, is based on expiation. Give me a righteousness, yet what becomes of the *sins* that I have committed? They must be washed out in blood for "without shedding of blood is no remission." That also I find in my Substitute.

> "For sins not His own
> He died to atone."

As the old Puritans put it, "Jesus was all His lifetime gathering and beating small the golden threads with which to weave the seamless robe of an imputed righteousness

THE DOCTRINES OF GRACE

and in His death He dipped that robe in the vermilion of His blood."

The Bible doctrine is that Christ makes up all liabilities, for us, to Godward. All, *all* our righteousnesses are but filthy rags and He is all our righteousness.

"By Him all who believe are justified from all things." The one act which saves us is a simple risk and venture upon Christ.

> "Upon a life I did not live,
> Upon a death I did not die,
> Another's death, Another's life,
> I risk my soul eternally."

The Bible proves itself to be Divine, because in it we have *God's thought* higher than man's thought; *His way* abolishing ours in salvation.

The Bible proves itself Divine because in it we are taught that we are saved out and out, by simple suspense on Another—that, to Godward, Christ is all in all and no man anything at all.

> "When He from His lofty throne,
> Stooped to do and die,
> Everything was fully done,
> Hearken to His cry.

> "*'It is finished!'* yes indeed,
> Finished every jot,
> Sinner, this is all you need
> Tell me, is it not?

> "Weary working plodding one,
> Wherefore toil you so?
> Cease your doing; all was done
> Long, long ago.

> "Till to Jesus' work you cling,
> By a simple faith,
> Doing is a deadly thing,
> Doing ends in death.

"Nothing either great or small,
  Nothing, sinner, *no,*
Jesus did it, did it all,
  Long, long ago.

"Cast your deadly 'doing' down,
  Down at Jesus' feet;
Stand in *Him,* in *Him alone,*
  Gloriously complete.

"When you know that you are saved,
  Trusting in the Blood,
You will live to Him who died,
  Yielded up to God.

"Gratitude is all our life,
  Merits none have we,
Filthy rags our righteousness,
  Christ alone our plea."

5. Now let us take a broader survey of the Scriptures and find still further confirmation of the fact that they are divine.

(1) Look at their *continuity.* "Not without Blood." A scarlet thread binds the Bible together from cover to cover. The Blood begins to flow at Eden's gate. It grows in mighty volume down the long line of sacrificial rites to Calvary. It gleams again in the "Lamb Slain" whom John beheld in the midst of the throne. Through every rope of the British navy there is twisted a single red cord. Cut any rope and you will find the cord. So through the 66 books of the Bible runs the Scarlet line of Atonement. Open any book and you will find a Bleeding Saviour. Revelation in its continuity and in its parts is one and the same.

(2) The Bible glimpses its Divinity in *unsuspected hints* and singular *coincidences.* Take for example, the 5th chapter of Genesis—a chapter which one might rashly call the dryest of genealogies. Yet there you get that sublimest pilgrimage and prophecy of Enoch and his wonderful trans-

lation, when he walked and walked with God until we see him walk *away* with God. More than this, the chapter in its very names gives us a forecast of redemption. *Adam,* "man made in the image of God"—*Seth,* "substituted by"—*Enos,* "man frail and sinful"—*Cainan,* yes and "sorrowing"—*Mahalaleel,* "the Blessed God"—*Jared,* "shall come down"—*Enoch,* "teaching"—*Methuselah,* "His death shall bring"—*Lamech,* "the despairing"—*Noah,* "consolation."

(3) Again—the Scope and Final Teaching of the Book is to reveal and justify a *Secret Providence.*

The teaching of the world's literature is pessimistic—Virtue suffers and is always struggling but at the last is defeated,—Circumstances—Fate overcomes her.

What can be sadder for example than the last interview of Hector and Andromache pictured by Homer at the Scean Gate of Troy?

This scene has been eulogized by classic scholars as one of the noblest ever painted in words—Yet look at it. Hector is to go out upon the field of battle—probably to die. "Oh Hector," sobs Andromache, "you are my all—more than father or dear mother or brothers and sisters whom I have lost in this terrible war. What shall I do if you fall?" Hector replies—"Yes I shall fall and you will be carried away captive and will be a slave to draw water in a far away land. I shall not help you for I shall be in my tomb." "But, Hector, what shall I do?" "You must go home and occupy yourself with household cares. These will help to distract you—They are your best comfort—Meanwhile we are in the hands of a relentless fate."

That is man's view of life—The view of all the Greek tragedies, Euripides, Sophocles, Eschylus—It is the view of 9 out of 10 of all our modern novels—even though they are written under the light of the Gospel. "It is of no use—Cheating prospers. The good man goes to the wall—The right-minded girl succumbs beneath too great a temptation. Righteousness may reign but not in *this one*—in some *other* world."

Now take the Bible view-point—Evil may succeed for a moment—but the devil is cast down—Adam falls but falls to rise again to bliss immortal—David flees as a partridge to the mountains but all the while is on the way to the throne

—Messiah suffers—but before Him is the prospect of unutterable triumph.

The Bible makes the future of those who trust in God a glorious, shining way that "shineth more and more"—"Weeping may endure for a *night* but joy cometh in the morning."

> "Let him who sows in sadness wait
> Till the fair harvest come
> He shall confess his sheaves are great
> And shout his harvest home."

God will wipe away all tears from all eyes—God will bring light out of darkness—meat out of the Eater—honey from the Rock. "God will help me if I fight his battles, and He will bring me back crowned with honors to your dear arms—Christ will be with you and we are always His!" This what the Christian Hector says to his weeping Andromanche.

A secret Providence! How beautifully Calvin wrote of a Secret Providence!

Take Joseph—Had he not been cast into the pit, he would not have been sold into Egypt—Had he not been thrown into prison he would never have interpreted the Butler's dream nor gone into the presence of Pharaoh nor have made the Second Ruler in the Land of Egypt.

Take Esther—Had not Haman thrown the lot for Adar 12 months ahead the Jews would have been cut off before the King's posts could countermand the decree—Had not King Ahasuerus had a sleepless night, Mordecai's service would never have been recognized nor would he have supplanted Haman in the affairs of Persia—and there would have been no *Purim* which the Jews observe to this day.

Secret Providence—"I will bring the blind by a way that they know not—I will make darkness light before them and crooked things straight. All things are working together for good to them that love God"—Oh Divine Book—Oh Peerless Revelation—"When I went into the Sanctuary then *understood* I, their *end.*"

THE TESTIMONY OF THE SCRIPTURE TO ITSELF

Hos. viii:12

"I have written to him the great things of My Law."

The Bible is the very handwriting of God! Suppose I believe that. Suppose, instead of Luke and John and Paul and Peter, I behold in overawed imagination "God grasping the pen" and setting down the sentences, the words, the jots and tittles—every stroke of it; does not that fix me? does not that arrest me? does not that determine, shape, and mould me, as no conviction other, lesser, can?

That is the Anchor to which, by twisting a few honest strands, I would help, if I may, to rebind our cables. When we were resting quietly inside of Sandy Hook, our own ship and others swung round with the tide, but none changed its place, for all were well anchored. The ships of sentiment are swinging loose to-day, and with the counter tide. That has been, and it will be, again and again, so long as human opinion is the vacillating and uncertain thing it is. But we need not fear, for the old anchor holds as firm, as steady, as inflexible as even That anchor—back of all departures, heresies, and fluctuations—is the literal, direct, Divine inspiration, *on the original parchments,* of the Word of God.

We cannot consent to see in the Bible the pens nor the penmen; but, undistractedly, the Master Intellect, which everywhere directs each thought. We must maintain with Justin Martyr, with Chrysostom, and with Theophilus of Antioch, the illustration of that *"harp"* on which the Spirit breathes, "the strings of which He touches to evoke each vital tone." We must "adore" with Athenogoras "the Being who has harmonized the strains, who leads the melody, and not the instrument on which He plays. What umpire at the Games," he cries, "omits the Minstrel while he crowns the lyre?"

The mistake of moderns, and especially of recent moderns, has been "crowning the lyre." The whole question of Inspiration has, within the last half century, been made to turn upon the *writers*. It has been unhinged from those stanchions on which St. Paul makes it turn—the *Writings themselves*.

This misdirection of thought would seem to be much like that of the boy who stands at the end of the telegraph line and gets a message from his father ("I have written to him the great things of My Law"), and who, instead of taking the message as direct, authoritative, final, goes to work to discuss the posts, the wires, electricity, the key-board, the touch of the finger, the process. His business is simply to heed and obey.

The doctrine of direct, dictated, verbal Inspiration—that everything in the Bible was set down by the finger of God—has these five things in its favor:

1. It is the *first*, original, and oldest doctrine.
2. It is the *simplest* doctrine.
3. It is the *undeviating* doctrine which has proved the bulwark of the Church of God. Defended in the earliest centuries by men like Athenagoras and St. Augustine —defended still by men like Wickliffe, Huss, and Luther in the struggles which led in the Reformation—and, in post-Reformation times, defended by men like the Buxtorfs, John Owen, John Gill, and Gaussen—it has been the one, consistent, inexpugnable, permanent doctrine from the beginning. Scripture—sunlight to the sun—is the untarnishable radiance of God. What *it* says, *God* says.
4. A fourth fact is the *logical impossibility* of any other counter position. "If we do not take direct Inspiration," says Waller, "what we are to take is not so clear." If we begin to admit inequalities in Revelation, where shall we stop? If we turn our attention away from the writing to occupy ourselves with the writer—his genius, his knowledge, the amount of assistance required—who does not see that this descent from heaven to earth, from the high Himalaya of the Divine to the low, marshy ground of the creatural human, must tend to gravitate, to minimize, and more and more, until your Bible is reduced to Shakespeare or (who

knows?) to Bret Harte. The fabricators of degrees in Inspiration—the men who so self-confidently set forth to us their four classes,—the inspirations of "elevation," of "superintendence," of "suggestion," of "direct dictation,"—tell us themselves that the last is the highest. Ah well! we will choose—we will cling to that highest. Why not? If dictation anywhere—in any one instance, then dictation all the way through. If not, why not? Where are the limits? Where shall we stop? Suppose certain words in the Scripture—only a few—to be put there by God. Suppose this admitted, and it is admitted—who shall define the number of those words? Who shall assume to stand up and tell us where God the Holy Ghost expresses Himself in the very form of the word and where He retires from the word and leaves it a shell merely human?

The difficulties attaching to any other view of Inspiration than the Verbal are simply overwhelming. Suppose that something, no matter how little—whatever you please—be left to the writers themselves, and who shall satisfy us that nothing essential has been omitted, nothing irrelevant or trifling has been emphasized, nothing inaccurate has been set down? Who does not see that, *so,* inspiration is utterly lost?

5. And that leads, logically, up to the climacteric position, that we must hold to Verbal Inspiration, or if not, at last—*give up the Bible.* What other result can there be? Is not this just what it comes back to—"I receive what appeals to my likings, I repudiate what I dislike?" In other words, I make my consciousness my arbiter; my prejudice, my Book; and my self-will, my God.

The subject which has fallen to my lot in this discussion* is, The Testimony of the Scriptures to themselves—their own self-evidence—the overpowering, unparticipated witness that they bring.

Permit me to expand this witness under the following heads:

---

*This discourse was first delivered in Philadelphia at an interdenominational conference in which the author represented the Dutch Reformed Church.

I. Immortality.
II. Authority.
III. Transcendent Doctrine.
IV. Direct Assertion.
V. The Casket of the Gem—the very Language in which Revelation is enshrined.

I. *Immortality—"I have written!"* All other books die. "Most of the libraries are cemeteries of dead books." The vast perennial literature falls as the leaves fall, and perishes as they perish. Few old books survive, and fewer of those that survive have any influence. Even to scholars the names of Epictetus and Lucretius—of the Novum Organum—of the Nibelungen Lied, convey nothing more than a title. They have heard of those books—have skimmed a page or two here and there,—that is all. Most of the books we quote from have been written within the last three or even one hundred years.

But here is a book whose antemundane voices had grown old, when voices spake in Eden. A book which has survived not only with continued but increasing lustre, vitality, vivacity, popularity, rebound of influence. A book which avalanches itself with accretions, like the snowball that packs as it goes. A book which comes through all the shocks without a wrench, and all the furnaces of all the ages—like an iron safe—with every document in every pigeon-hole, without a warp upon it, or the smell of fire. Here is a book of which it may be said, as of Immortal Christ Himself—"Thou hast the dew of thy youth from the womb of the morning." A book dating from days as ancient as those of the Ancient of Days—and which, when all that makes up what we see and call the universe shall be dissolved, will still speak on in thunder-tones of majesty, and whisper-tones of light and music-tones of love—for it is wrapping in itself the everlasting past—and opening and expanding from itself the everlasting future: and, like an all-irradiating sun, will still roll on, while deathless ages roll, the one unchanging, unchangeable Revelation of God.

II. Immortality is on these pages, and *Authority sets here her seal. This is the second point, a Standard.*

Useless to talk about *no* standard. Nature points to one. Conscience cries out for one—conscience which without a law constantly wages the internal and excruciating war of accusing or else excusing itself.

There must be a Standard and an Inspired Standard—for *Inspiration is the Essence of Authority,* and authority is in proportion to Inspiration—the more Inspired the greater the authority—the less, the less. Even the rationalist Rothe, a most intense opponent, has admitted that *"that* in the Bible which is not the product of direct inspiration has no binding power."

Verbal and direct Inspiration is, therefore, the "Thermopylæ" of Biblical and Scriptural faith. No breath, no syllable; no syllable, no word; no word, no Book; no Book, no religion.

We hold, from first to last, that there can be no possible advance in Revelation—no new light. What was written at first, the same thing stands written to-day, and will stand forever. The Bible, the true fact beneath the Grecian myth, springs into light Minerva-like, full armed. The emanation of the mind of God—it is complete, perfect. "Nothing can be put to it, nor anything taken from it." Its *ipse dixit* is peremptory—final. What can be more awful, more stupendous than the sanction which rounds up the Book, by which it is secured and sealed and guarded? "If any man shall add unto these things, God shall add unto him the plagues that are written in this Book: and if any man shall *take away from the words* of the Book of this prophecy, God shall take away his part out of the Book of life, and out of the Holy City, and from the things which are written in this Book."

The Bible IS the Word of God, and not simply CONTAINS it. This is clear,—

Because all the words in it, even those of the Devil and of wicked men, were put down by the finger of God.

Because the Bible styles itself the Word of God. *"The Word of the Lord* is right," says the Psalmist. Again, *"Thy Word* is a lamp to my feet." "Wherewithal shall a young man cleanse his way? By taking heed thereto according to *Thy Word."* "The grass withereth," says Isaiah, "the flower thereof fadeth, but *the Word of our God* shall stand forever."

Not only is the Bible called the Word of God, but it is distinguished from all other books by that very title. It is so distinguished in the 119th Psalm, and everywhere the contrast between it and every human book is deepened and sustained.

If we will not call the Bible the Word of God, then we cannot call it anything else. If we insist upon a description rigorously exact and unexposed to shafts of wanton criticism, then the Book remains anonymous. We cannot more consistently say "Holy Scripture," because the crimes recorded on its pages are not holy; because expressions like "Curse God and die," and others from the lips of Satan and of wicked men, are unholy. The Bible, however, is "holy," because its records are true and its aim and its methods are holy. The Bible, likewise, is the Word of God, because it comes from God; because its every word was penned by God; because it is the only exponent of God, the only rule of His procedure, and the Book by which we must at last be judged.

1. The Bible is authority because in it, from cover to cover, *God is the speaker.* Said a leader of our so-called orthodoxy to a crowded audience but a little while ago: "The Bible is true. Any man not a fool must believe what is true. What difference does it make who wrote it?"

This difference, brethren: *the solemn bearing down of God on the soul!* My friend may tell me what is true; my wife may tell me what is true; but what they say is not solemn. Solemnity comes in when God looks into my face—God! and behind Him everlasting destiny—and talks with me about my soul. In the Bible GOD speaks, and GOD is listened to, and men are born again by God's Word. "He is not a Christian who believes or obeys Matthew or John or Peter or Paul." What makes a Christian is believing and obeying God. "So then Faith cometh by hearing, and hearing by the Word of God." It is *God's* Revelation that faith hears, and it is *on God revealed* that faith rests.

THE DOCTRINES OF GRACE

2. The Bible is the Word of God. It comes to us *announced by miracles and heralded with fire*. Take the Old Testament—Mt. Sinai; take the New Testament—Pentecost. Would God himself stretch out His hand and write on tables in the giving, and send down tongues of fire for the proclamation of a Revelation, every particle and shred of which was not His own? In other words, would He work miracles and send down tongues of fire to signalize a work merely human, or even partly human and partly Divine? How unworthy of God, how impious, how utterly impossible the supposition!

3. The Bible comes clothed with authority in the *high-handed and exalted terms of its address*. God in the Bible speaks out of a whirlwind and with the voice of Elias. What grander proof of literal inspiration can be than in the high-handed method and imperative tone of prophets and apostles which enabled them—poor men, obscure, and without an influence; fishermen, artisans, publicans, day-laborers—to brave and boldly teach the world from Pharaoh and from Nero down? Was this due to anything less than God speaking in them—to the overpowering impulse and seizure of God? Who can believe it? Who is not struck with the power and the wisdom of God? "His words were in my bones," cries one. "I could not stay. The lion hath roared, who will not fear; the Lord hath spoken, who can but prophesy?"

4. The Bible is the optime of authority, because it is from first to last a glorious projection on the widest scale of the *decrees of God*. The sweep of the Bible is from the Creation of Angels to a new heaven and new earth, across a lake of fire. What a field for events! what an expanse beyond the sweep or even reach of human forethought, criticism, or co-operation! what a labyrinth upon whose least, minutest turning hangs entire redemption, since a chain is never stronger than its smallest link! Who, then, will dare to speak till God has spoken? "I will declare the decree!" That pushes everything aside—that makes the declaration an extension, so to say, of the Declarer. "I will declare the decree!" When we consider that **the Bible is an exact projection of the decrees of God into**

the future, this argument is seen to lift, indeed, to a climax; and, in fact, it does reach to the very *Crux* of controversy; for the hardest thing for us to believe about God is to believe that He exactly absolutely knows, because He has ordained, the future. Every attribute of God is easier to grasp than that of an infallible Omniscience. "I will declare the decree," therefore, calls for direct inspiration.

5. The Bible is the optime of authority, because *the Hooks at the end of the chain prove the dictated Inspiration of its every link*. Compare the Fall in Genesis—(one link), with the Resurrection in the Apocalypse—the other. Compare the Old Creation in the first chapters of the Old Testament with the New Creation in the last chapters of the New. "We open the first pages of the Bible," says Valloton, "and we find there the recital of the creation of the world by the word of God—of the fall of man, of his exile from God—far from Paradise, and far far from the tree of life. We open the last pages of the last of the 66 books dating 4,000 years later. God is still speaking. He is still creating. He creates a new heaven and a new earth. Man is found there recovered. He is restored to communion with God. He dwells again in Paradise, beneath the shadow of the tree of life. Who is not struck by the strange correspondence of this end with that beginning? Is not the one the prologue, the other the epilogue of a drama as vast as unique?"

6. The Bible is the optime of authority, because, over this vast range of supernatural, confessedly Divine thought, purpose, and action, there are no lights, and *no explanations, save those furnished by the Book itself*. That Book must be supreme, whose only parallel, comparison, and confirmation is itself. Here is an *argumentum ad hominem*. Why do we not possess concordances for other volumes—for their very words? Because in human writings there is no such nicety—no such Divine significance as makes the sense and all the argument turn on the single words, and their exact consistency and correspondence everywhere throughout the book. Your concordance, my brother, every time you take it up, speaks loudly to you of the inspiration and authority of Holy Writ. It says to you: "Not the

THE DOCTRINES OF GRACE

Bible only, but this word, that word—all these single words, are God-breathed—Divine!"

7. Another argument for the supreme authority of Scripture, is the *character of the investigation challenged* for the Word of God. The Bible courts the closest scrutiny. Its open pages blaze the legend: "Search the Scriptures!" *Ereunao*—"Search." It is a sportsman's term, and borrowed from the chase. "Trace out"—"track out"—follow the word in all its usages and windings. Scent it out to its remotest meaning, as a dog the hare. "They searched," again says St. Luke, in the Acts, of the Bereans. There it is another word, *anakrino*, "they divided up," analyzed, sifted, pulverized, as in a mortar—to the last thought.

What a solemn challenge is this! What book but a Divine Book would dare speak such a challenge? If a book has been written by man, it is at the mercy of men. Men can go through it, riddle it, sift it, and leave it behind them, worn out. But the Bible, a Book dropped from heaven, is "God-breathed." It swells, it dilates, with the bodying fullness of God. God has written it, and none can exhaust it. Apply your microscopes, apply your telescopes to the material of Scripture. They separate, but do not fray, its threads. They broaden out its nebulæ, but find them clustered stars. They do not reach the hint of poverty in Scripture. They nowhere touch on coarseness in the fabric, nor on limitations in horizon, as always is the case when tests of such a character are brought to bear on any work of man's. You put a drop of water, or a fly's wing, under a microscope. The stronger the lens, the more that drop of water will expand, till it becomes an ocean filled with sporting animalcules. The higher the power, the more exquisite, the more silken become the tissues of the fly's wing, until it attenuates almost to the golden and gossamer threads of a seraph's. So is it with the Word of God. The more scrutiny, the more divinity; the more dissection, the more perfection. We cannot bring to it a test too penetrating, nor a light too lancinating, nor a touchstone too exacting.

The Bible is beyond all attempts at exhaustion, not only, but comprehension. No human mind can, by searching, find out the fullness of God. "For what man knoweth the things of a man save the spirit of man which is in him? even so the things of God knoweth no man save the Spirit of God."

III. That leads up to the third point. The Scriptures testify to their Divine Original *by their transcendent doctrine, their outshining light, their native radiance, the glow of the Divine, the witness of the Spirit.*

We should expect to find a Book, that came from God, pencilled with points of jasper and of sardine stone—enhaloed with a brightness from the everlasting hills. We should look for that about the book which, flashing conviction at once, should *carry* overwhelmingly and everywhere, by its bare, naked witness—by what it simply is. That, just as God, by stretching out a hand to write upon the "plaister" of a Babylonian palace, stamped, through mysterious and disjointed words, conviction of Divinity upon Belshazzar and each one of his one thousand "lords," so, after that same analogue,—why not?—God should stretch out His hand along the unrolling palimpsests of all ages, and write upon them *larger* words, which, to the secret recognition of each human soul should say, not only, "This is Truth," but "This is Truth, God-spoken!"

A Book of Infinites

The Bible is the Word of God, because it is the *Book of Infinites*—the Revelation of what nature, without it, never could have attained, and, coming short of the knowledge of which, nature were lost.

The greatest need of the soul is salvation. It is such a knowledge of God as shall assure us of "comfort" here and hereafter. Such knowledge, nature, outside of the Bible, does not contain. Everywhere groping in his darkness, man is confronted by two changeless facts. One, his guilt, which, as he looks down, sinks deeper and deeper. The other, the Justice of God, which, as he looks up, lifts higher and higher. Infinite against Infinite—Infinite here; Infinite there—no bridge between them! Nature helps to no bridge. It nowhere speaks of Atonement.

Standing with Uriel in the sun, we launch the proposition

that the Scriptures are Divine in their very message because they deal with three Infinites:—Infinite Guilt; Infinite Holiness; Infinite Atonement.

A Book must itself be *infinite* which deals with Infinites; and a Book must be *Divine* which divinely reconciles Infinites.

Infinite Guilt! Has my guilt any bottom? Is Hell any deeper? Is there, in introspection, a possible lower, more bottomless nadir? Infinite Guilt! That is what opens, caves away under my feet, the longer, the more carefully I plumb my own heart—my nature, my record. Infinitely guilty! That is what I am and *where*—far, far below the plane of self-apology, or ghastly "criticism" of the Book which testifies to this. Infinitely guilty! That is what I am. Infinitely sinking, and, below me, an infinite Tophet. I know that. As soon as the Bible declares it, I know it, and, with it, I know that witnessing Bible divine. I know it—I do not know how—by an instinct, by conscience, by illumination, by the power of the Spirit of God; by the Word without, and by the flashed conviction in me which accord.

And counterpoised above, me, a correlative Infinite—God! What can be higher? What zenith loftier? What doming of responsibility more dread or more portentous? Infinite God—above me—coming to judge me! On the way now. I must meet Him. I know that. I know it, as soon as the Bible declares it. I know it—I do not know how—by an instinct. Even the natural man must picture to himself when thus depicted, and must fear,

"A God in grandeur, and a world on fire."

An infinitely Holy God above me, coming to judge me. That is the Second Infinite.

Then the Third and what completes the Triangle, and makes its sides eternally, divinely equal—Infinite Atonement—an Infinite Saviour—God on the cross making answer to God on the throne—my Jesus—my refuge—my Everlasting Jehovah.

By these three Infinites—especially this last—this infinite Atonement, for which my whole being cries out its last cry of exhaustion—by this third side of the stupendous Triangle—the side which, left to myself, I could never make out, the Bible proves itself the soul's Geometry—the one Eternal Mathematics—the true Revelation of God.

Aye! and by that ineffable something—self-luminous—flooding the soul, which bathing the Book bears the reader as well on its tide.

> La larga ploia
> Dello Spirito santo, ch'è diffusa
> In su le Vecchie e in su le nuove cuoia,
> É sillogismo, che la mi ha conchiusa
> Acutamente sì, che in verso d'ella
> Ogni dimostrazion mi pare ottusa.

> "The flood, I answered, of the Spirit of God
> Rained down upon the Ancient Testament and New,
> This is the reasoning that convinceth me
> So feelingly, each argument beside
> Seems blunt and forceless in comparison."*

We take the ground that these three things—Guilt, God, Atonement—set thus in star-like apposition and conjunction, *speak* from the sky, more piercingly than stars do, saying: "Sinner and sufferer, this Revelation is Divine!"

The Scriptures are their own self-evidence. The refusal of the Bible on its simple presentation, is enough to damn any man, and if persisted in, will damn him—for,

> "A glory gilds the sacred page,
> Majestic, like the sun,
> It gives a light to every age,
> It gives, but borrows none."

IV. Glory spreads over the face of the Scriptures, but this glory, when scrutinized closely, is seen to contain certain features and outlines—*testimonies inside of itself, direct assertions, which conspire to illustrate again its high Divinity, and to confirm its claim.*

This is our fourth point: The Scriptures say of themselves that they are Divine. They not only assume it; they say it.

---

*Dante—*Il Paradiso*.

And this, "Thus saith the Lord," is intrinsic—a witness inside of the witness, and one upon which something more than conviction—confidence, or Spirit-born and *saving faith,* depends.

The argument from the self-assertion of Scripture is cumulative.

1st. The Bible claims that, *as a Book,* it comes from God.

2d. It asserts that its very words are the words of God; that each pen-stroke is God-breathed—inspired.

Now, let us go back, and resume these two points a little more slowly; and,

1st. The Bible claims that, *as a Book,* it comes from God. In various ways, it urges this claim.

One thing; it says so. "God in old times spake by the prophets; God now speaks by His Son." The question of Inspiration is, in its first statement, the question of Revelation itself. If the Book be divine, then what it says of itself is Divine. The Scriptures are inspired because they say they are inspired. The question is simply one of Divine testimony, and our business is, as simply, to receive that testimony. "Inspiration is as much an assertion," says Haldane, "as is justification by faith. Both stand, and equally, on the authority of Scripture, which is as much an ultimate authority upon this point as upon any other." When God speaks, and when He says "I speak!" there is the whole of it. He is bound to be heard and obeyed. And God does speak. He brings the Bible to us, and He claims to be its Author. If, at this moment, yonder heavens were opened—the curtained canopy of star-sown clouds rolled back—if, amid the brightness of the light ineffable, the Dread Eternal were Himself seen, rising from His throne, and heard to speak to us in voices audible—no one of these could be more potent, more imperative, than what lies now before us upon Inspiration's page.

In the Bible, GOD speaks, and speaks not only by proxy. Leviticus is a signal example of this. Chapter after chapter of Leviticus begins: "And the Lord spake, saying;" and so it runs on through the chapter. Moses is simply a listener, a scribe. The self announced speaker is God,

In the Bible, God himself comes down and speaks, not in the Old Testament alone, and not alone by proxy. "The New Testament presents us," says Dean Burgon, "with the august spectacle of the Ancient of Days, holding the entire volume of the Old Testament Scriptures in His hands, and interpreting it of Himself. He, the Incarnate Word, 'who was in the beginning with God,' and 'who was God'—that same Almighty One is set forth in the Gospels as holding the 'volume of the Book' in His hands—as opening and unfolding it, and explaining it everywhere of Himself." Christ everywhere receives the Scriptures, and speaks of the Scriptures, in their entirety—the Law, the Prophets, and the Psalms, the whole Old Testament canon—as the living Oracle of God. He accepts and He endorses everything written, and even makes most prominent those miracles which infidelity regards as most incredible. And He does all this upon the ground of the authority of God. He passes over the writer—leaves him out of account. In all His quotations from the Old Testament, He mentions but four of the writers by name. The question with Him is not a question of the *reporter,* but of the Dictator. Suppose a sovereign like Kaiser Wilhelm dictating five or six letters to five or six different private secretaries at once. Suppose that six agents have penned the six parts of one letter! Our Saviour does not see the six pens. He sees the one Writer, the one Hand outstretched, viewless, infallible, awful—behind all human hands.

And this position of our Saviour which exalted Scripture as the mouthpiece of the living God was steadily maintained by the apostles and the apostolic Church. Again and over again, in the book of the Acts, in all the Epistles, do we find such expressions as "He saith," "God saith," "The oracles of God," "The Holy Ghost saith," "Well spake the Holy Ghost by Esaias the prophet."

The Epistle to the Hebrews furnishes a splendid illustration of this, where, setting forth the whole economy of the Mosaic rites, the author adds, "The Holy Ghost this signifying." Further on, and quoting words of Jeremiah, he enforces them with the remark, "The Holy Ghost is witness to us also." The imperial argument on Psalm xcv he clenches with the application, "Wherefore (as the Holy

Ghost saith), To-day if ye will hear His voice." Throughout the entire Epistle, whoever may have been the writer quoted from, the words of the quotation, are referred to God.*

2d. But now let us come closer, to the very exact and categorical and unequivocal assertion. If the Scriptures as a Book are Divine, then what they say of themselves is Divine. What do they say?

In this inquiry, let us keep our fingers on two words, and always on two words—the Apostolic keys to the whole Church position— γραφὴ θεόπνευστος "Graphe"—writing, writing, THE WRITING,—not somebody, something back of the Writing. The Writing, *"He Graphe,"* that was inspired.

And what is meant by inspired? *"Theopneustos,"* God-breathed. Modern theologians have played at shuttle-cock with various degrees of inspiration. It is indeed a wretched play—this bandying of quibbles in the mouths of mortals to whom God vouchsafes to speak, and who themselves are sitting shaking on the crumbling precipice of an Eternal destiny.

Degrees of inspiration! Shades of varying value in the cadences of the Almighty's voice! He whispers, hesitates, speaks low in Esther, in the sixteenth chapter of St. Mark, and in the eighth chapter of St. John's Gospel. He stutters, falters in the Genealogies; is inaccurate in figures. He evidently weakens, halts: Almighty God breaks down!

Degrees of inspiration! The older theologians, thank God; did not know them—nor own them. Why should they? As well discuss degrees in Deity, in Predestination, in Providence, as talk about degrees in that of which Augustine says: "Whatsoever He willed that we should read either of His doings or sayings, that He commissioned His agents to write, as if their hands had been His own hands."

"God breathed" sweeps the whole ground. God comes down as a blast on the pipes of an organ,—in voice like a whirlwind, or in still whispers like Aeolian tones, and saying the word, He seizes the hand, and makes that hand in His own the pen of a most ready writer.

Pasa Graphe Theopneustos! "All sacred writing." More

---
*Olshausen, Die Echtheit des N. T., cited by Dr. Lee.

exactly, "every sacred writing"—every mark on the parchment is "God-breathed." So says St. Paul.

Pasa Graphe Theopneustos! The sacred assertion is not of the instruments, but of the *Author;* not of the agents, but of the *Product.* It is the sole and sovereign *vindication of what has been left on the page when Inspiration gets through.* "What is written," says Jesus, "how readest thou?" Men can only read what is written.

Pasa Graphe Theopneustos! God inspires not men, but language. The phrase, "inspired men," is not found in the Bible. The Scripture never employs it. The Scripture says that "holy men were moved"—*pheromenoi*—but that their writing, their manuscript, what they put down and left on the page, was God-breathed. You breathe upon a pane of glass. Your breath congeals there; freezes there; stays there; fixes an ice-picture there. That is the notion. The writing on the page beneath the hand of Paul was just as much breathed on, breathed *into* that page, as was His soul breathed into Adam.

The Chirograph was God's incarnate voice, as truly as the flesh of Jesus sleeping on the "pillow" was incarnate God.

We take the ground that *on the original parchment*—the membrane—every sentence, word, line, mark, point, pen-stroke, jot, tittle, was put there by God.

On the *original parchment.* There is no question of other, anterior parchments. Even were we to indulge the violent extra-Scriptural notion that Moses or Matthew transcribed from memory or from other books the things they have left us; still, in any, in every such case, the selection, the expression, the shaping and turn of the phrase on the membrane was the work of an unaided God.

But what? Let us have done with extra-Scriptural, presumptuous suppositions. The burning Isaiah—the perfervid, wheel-gazing Ezekiel—the ardent, seraphic St. Paul, caught up, up, up into that Paradise which he himself calls the "third heaven"—were these men only "coypists," mere self-moved "redactors?" I trow not. Their pens urged, swayed, moved hither, thither by the sweep of a heavenly current, stretched their feathered tops, like that of Luke upon St. Peter's dome, into the far-off Empyrean—winged from the throne of God.

We take the ground that *on the original parchment, the membrane, every sentence, word, line, mark, point, pen-stroke, jot, tittle, was put there by God.*

On the original parchment. Men may destroy that parchment. Time may destroy it. To say that the membranes have suffered in the hands of men, is but to say that everything Divine must suffer, as the pattern Tabernacle suffered, when committed to our hands. To say, however, that the *writing* has suffered—the words and letters—is to say that Jehovah has failed.

The writing remains. Like that of a palimpsest, it will survive and reappear, no matter what circumstances,—what changes come in to scatter, obscure, disfigure, or blot it away. Not even one lonely "Theos*" writ large by the Spirit of God on the Great Uncial "C" as, with my own eyes I have seen it—plain, vivid, glittering, outstarting from behind the pale and overlying ink of Ephraem the Syrian—can be buried. Like Banquo's ghost, it will rise; and God himself replace it, and, with a hammer-stroke, beat down deleting hands. The parchments, the membranes decay; the writings, the words are eternal as God. Strip off the plaster from Belshazzar's palace, yet Mene! Mene! Tekel! Upharsin! remain. They *remain*.

Let us go through them, and from the beginning, and see what the Scriptures say of themselves.

One thing: they say that God spake, πάλαι ἐν τοῖς προφήταις "anciently and all the way down, *in* the prophets." One may make, if he pleases, the ἐν instrumental—as it is more often instrumental—*i. e., "by"* the prophets; but in either case, *in* them, or *by* them, the Speaker was God.

Again: the Scriptures say that the laws the writers promulgated, the doctrines they taught, the stories they recorded—above all, their prophecies of Christ, were not their own; were not originated, nor conceived by them,—were not rehearsed, by them, from memory, nor obtained from any outside sources—were not what they had any means, before, of knowing, or of comprehending, but were

---

*"God" was manifest in the flesh, 1 Tim. 16.

immediately from God; they themselves being only recipient, only concurrent with God, as God moved upon them.

Some of the speakers of the Bible, as Balaam, the Old Prophet of Bethel, Caiaphas, are seized and made to speak in spite of themselves; and, with the greatest reluctance, to utter what is farthest from their minds and hearts. Others —in fact all—are purblind to the very oracles, instructions, visions, they announce. "Searching what, or what manner of time, the Spirit of Christ which was in them did signify!" *i. e.*, the prophets themselves did not know what they wrote. What picture can be more impressive than that of the prophet himself hanging over and contemplating in surprise, in wonder, in amazement, his own autograph—as if it had been left upon the table there—the relict of some strange and supernatural Hand? How does that picture lift away the Bible from all human hands and place it back, as His original Deposit, in the hands of God.

Again: it is said that "the Word of the Lord came" to such and such a writer. It is not said that the SPIRIT came, which is true; but that the *Word* itself came, the Dabar-Jehovah. And it is said: *"Hayo Haya Dabar,"* that it *substantially* came—essentially came *"essendo fuit"*—so say Pagninus, Montanus, Polanus—*i. e.*, it came germ, seed and husk and blossom—in its totality—*"words* which the Holy Ghost teacheth"—the "words."

Again: it is *denied,* and most emphatically, that the words are the words of the man—of the agent. "The Spirit of the Lord," says David, "spake by me, and His word was in my tongue." St. Paul asserts that *"Christ spake in him"* (2 Cor. xiii:3). "Who hath made man's mouth? Have not I, the Lord? I will put *my* words into thy mouth." That looks very much like what has been stigmatized as the "mechanical theory." It surely makes the writer a mere organ, although not an unconscious, or unwilling, unspontaneous organ. Could language more plainly assert or defend a verbal direct inspiration?

Yes, but in only one way—*i. e.*, by denying the agent. And that denial we equally have from the lips of our Saviour. *"It is not ye that speak,* but the Spirit of your Father which speaketh in you. Take no thought *how* or *what* ye shall say. The Holy Ghost shall teach you what ye *ought* to say"—both the "how" and the "what"—both the matter and form.

In a line with the fact, again it is said that the word came to the writers without any study—*"suddenly"* as to Amos (chap. vii:15), where he is taken from following the flock.

Again: When the word thus came to the prophets *they had not the power to conceal it.* It was "like a fire in their bones" which must speak or write, as Jeremiah says, or consume its human receptacle.

And to make this more clear, it is said that holy men were *pheromenoi*, "moved" or rather carried along in a supernatural, ecstatic current—a *delectatio scribendi*. They were not left one instant to their wit, wisdom, fancies, memories, or judgments either to order, or arrange, or dispose, or write out. They were *only reporters*, intelligent, conscious, passive, plastic, docile, exact, and accurate reporters. They were like men who wrote with different kinds of ink. They colored their work with tints of their own personality, or rather God colored it, having made the writer as the writing, and the writer for that special writing; and because the work ran *through them* just as the same water, running through glass tubes, yellow, green, red, violet, will be yellow, violet and green, and red.

God wrote the Bible, the whole Bible, and the Bible as a whole. He wrote each word of it, as truly as He wrote the Decalogue on the Tables of stone.

Higher criticism tells us—the "New Departure" tells us, that *Moses* was inspired, but the *Decalogue* not. But Exodus and Deuteronomy, seven times over, declare that God stretched down the tip of His finger from heaven and left the *marks*, the gravements, the cut characters, the scratches on the stones (Exod. xxiv:12). "I will give thee Tables of stone, commandments, *which I have written*" (Exod. xxxi:18). "And He gave unto Moses, upon Mount Sinai, two tables of testimony, tables of stone *written with the finger of God*" (Exod. xxxii:16). "The Tables were the work of God and *the writing was the writing of* God, graven upon the tables" (Deut. iv:12, 13). "The Lord spake unto you out of the midst of the fire, and He declared unto you His covenant, even ten commandments, and *He wrote them* upon two tables of stone" (Deut. v:22). "These words the Lord spake and *He wrote them* in two Tables of stone and delivered them unto me" (Deut. ix:10). "And the Lord delivered unto me two Tables of stone *written with the finger of God!*"

Seven times, and to men to whom writing is instinct; to beings who are most of all impressed, not by vague vanishing voices, but by words arrested, fixed, set down; and who themselves cannot resist the impulse to commit their own words to some written deposit, even of stone, or of bark, if they have not the paper; seven times, to men, to whom writing is instinct and who are inclined to rely for their highest conviction on what they have styled "documentary evidence," *i. e.*, on books;—God comes in and declares, "I have written!"

The Scriptures, whether with the human instrument or without the human instrument, with Moses or without Moses, were written by God. When God had finished, Moses had nothing else to do but carry down God's autograph. That is our doctrine. The Scriptures, if ten words, then all the words—if the Law, then the Gospels—the writing, the writings, *He Graphe—Hai Graphai*—expressions repeated more than fifty times in the New Testament alone—*this, these* were inspired.

V. And so we reach the fifth and closing head—the Casket of the Gem. The Bible is its own self evidence, not only in its Immortality—in its sublime Authority—in its transcendent Doctrine—in its direct assertions; but *also in the very* Languages in which it is enshrined.

Let us go back to the Hebrew—to God's language—to the tongue in which He said, "Let there be light!" before there was a world.

The oldest languages are philologically the most perfect, and nothing else, perhaps, betrays so deep, so pathetic a stamp of the Fall as does the downward progress of the human tongue.

Back of our coarser and more block-like English, we transfer ourselves to the French, with its subtler refinements—with touches of its hair-like pencillings upon the shades of thought; or with its buoyant swell and give to all emotion, as elasticities of wave to sinuosities of shore.

THE DOCTRINES OF GRACE

And back of this again: in dream-like thrall to more melodious cadences of the Italian tones—"accents whose law was beauty, and whose breath enrapturing music." And back of these—back of their mother-Latin—to the infinite versatility and grandeur and depth and comprehensiveness of the Greek. Greek! in itself a universe prepared for teeming and for populating thought. Greek! with its infinite and wondrous subtleties of shade in mood and tense, its play of graceful and innumerable particles, and cadences like chimes of air-flung and metallic bells. And, back, still back—and, the farther, the more complicated and abstruse—the more exacting in its constructions—the more precise in its articulations—the more attenuated in its case and tense endings, is our human speech—the more Divine a vehicle of wide enfranchised thought. The Sanscrit is not any longer like pulley-blocks roped together, nor like corals threaded on a string. Smooth and pellucid in its flow, it is as liquid sunlight dropping in echoes of a rhythmic and remote cascade, as from the ledges of an upper and angelic heaven.

Language, then, the higher we trace it, is not found to be a bungling and mechanical attempt at understanding. It is more and more the throb of holy heart to heart— the flash of heavenly thought rekindling thought, without the chasmed break, without the filmy veil; and all our dying tongues, down to the latest, are but fainter echoes—fragments of that earlier and loftier speech, in which the angels spoke to man—Adam to God, and God to Adam. When we have reached the beginning, we have in possession the *language* of God; the *words* and the GRAMMAR which God gave in Eden—which man has corrupted, confounded, lost away in dialectic dislocations since the fall.

The Hebrew, like a prism shattered into various lights at Babel, is the matrix of all other roots and forms.

1. Because in it, as in no other, names are Divinely expressive. Originally, names are characters in photograph. They are, or they should be, like labels on phials, which describe the contents. Names at the first were manifestations of men and of things. They are so in Hebrew. Adam means "Earthy," Seth "Substituted," Noah "The Con-

soler," Abraham "The Father of Multitudes," Jacob "Supplanter," Moses "Delivered," "Drawn out."

2. The Hebrew is original, because in it, as in no other, derivatives are built upon their roots, so that one can look through the derivative straight to the root, or back, so to say, though the slides of the telescope to the first slide—the root notion ruling unswervingly everywhere. Take as an example, Adam—earthy, because made from the earth—Isha, "woman," because made from Ish, man. In other languages the continuity is often broken. In Greek, *anthropos,* "man," has no relation to *ge,* the earth. In Latin, *mulier,* or *femina,* "woman," has no relation to *homo.*

3. The Hebrew form is antecedent to all similar forms in all other languages. Its root stands first. This is splendidly argued by Scaliger in opposition to the Maronites, who claimed a greater antiquity for the Syriac. What is the Syriac for "King," says Scaliger,—MELEKAH." What is the Hebrew?—"MELEK." Which has the root, and which is the shorter? That settles it.

4. Because the language employed by Adam in naming the animals was Hebrew, and that language was not invented by him upon the occasion, but had been taught him by God.

One thing: Because the names given to the animals imply a knowledge of their attributes and characteristics.

Another thing: God had already been talking to Adam, and in the same language.

Again: It seems that the animals were brought to Adam as object-lessons, to see what he could call them—*i. e.,* God wished to see how accurately Adam would fit the name taught to the thing.

5. Because language is called in Scripture, not only *"Throat"* and *"Lip,"* but especially *"Tongue;"* and it is said that God teaches man this: "The Lord God hath given me the tongue of the learned" (Isa.1:4). "The preparations of the heart," not only, but *"the answer of the tongue,* is from the Lord."

6. Because the whole earth was once of one tongue and one speech, and that speech by common consent of all Jewish and Gentile Traditions, the Lingua Sancta, the Holy, or the Hebrew Tongue. So says Ephodeus; so Jonathan the

Paraphrast. With this agree the Kabbalists, the Jerusalem Talmud, the Book of Cosri, R. Ben Jarchi, R. Ben Ezra, R. Levi ben Gerson—as well as Jerome, Ambrose, Chrysostom, Augustine.*

7. Because God himself spoke before Adam was created, and spoke in Hebrew, calling "Light," יוֹם Day; "Darkness," לַיְלָה Night; "Firmament," שָׁמַיִם Heaven; "Dry land," אֶרֶץ Earth, etc.

Hebrew was the first language, and therefore the most perfect language; for "that which is perfect," says Aristotle, "requires a perfect expression"; and Adam, being made very good, must have had a language *very, i. e.,* perfectly good; besides, a language which God speaks, must be like God.

Thus, stamped upon the gravements of its very *casket*—upon the very tongues in which it speaks, we read conspicuous, *self-evident,* the truth, that while Philosophy, the science of man, moves forward, Theology, the science of God, moves backward—"Philosophia quotidie *pro*-gressu, Theologia nisi *re*-gressu non crescit."

Backward, backward, backward, the whole Volume moves us—not only nineteen centuries behind the present moment; but back of time itself and every moment into the light of all eternities—to speak the proclamation of a Gospel as antique and as unchangeable as are the determinate counsel and the foreknowledge of God—for "Of Him and through Him and to Him, are all things— to whom be the glory, forever. Amen!"

Brethren: the danger of our present day—the "downgrade," as it has been called, of doctrine, of conviction, of the moral sentiment—a decline more constantly patent, as it is more blatantly proclaimed, does it not find its first step in our lost hold upon the very inspiration of the Word of God?

Does not a fresh conviction here, lie at the root of every remedy which we desire, as its sad lack lies at the root of every ruin we deplore?

Brethren: a fresh conviction—only that—*of the very Inspiration* of the Word of God—spreading itself abroad

*See Buxtorf, *"De Antiquitate Ling. Heb."*

in the minds of our earnest American people, would wake —from Maine to Arizona, and from Florida to Idaho—the wave of a revival such as this continent has never known.

Key up! then—let us key up our *"Credo"* in the absoluteness of the word which God has spoken. Bind again! Let us re-bind all cables to that Anchor, and the Ship of destiny, including all souls' freightage, will again obey her rudder, and be saved from wreck.

The great question for every man is that of his personal answer to the Word, spoken out of the skies, of a personal God.

THE INSPIRATION OF THE HEBREW LETTERS AND VOWEL-POINTS

St. Matt. v:18

"For verily I say unto you, Till heaven and earth pass away, one jot or one tittle shall in no wise pass from the law till all be fulfilled."

The question as to literal and chirographic inspiration will always move back inch by inch in discussion, until it has reached and finally confronted the crucial defense of the Reformers—THAT OF THE VERY POINTS.

The New Testament hangs for authority upon the Old Testament, and the Old Testament hangs upon the Points.

It is perfectly well understood by us all that the consonants are characters or letters in the Hebrew, and that the vowels are placed over these, within them, but especially *beneath* them in the form of marks or points.

These points determine the words, and the words determine the sentence. Whether a word be a noun or a verb; or, if a noun, what noun? if a verb, what verb? passive or active, past, present, or future?—all this, in a given particular case, may depend on the points.

Take as an illustration, in the Hebrew the word שָׂעַר *to esteem*. This, by change of the vowels, becomes שַׁעַר *a gate*; שֹׁעֵר *a porter*; שָׁעָר *vile*; שָׂעַר *to shudder*; שֵׂעָר *the hair*; שַׂעַר *fear, horror*. All seven words, verb, noun, or adjective, to be distinguished only by the points.

Take as another illustration, in the English, the word "Broad," for instance. The consonants are B. R. D. Now for the vowels—*Bard, Bird, Beard, Board, Aboard, Brad, Braid, Bred*, past of to breed—*Bread*, an article of food—*Broad, Abroad, Brood*. Twelve words, at least with three consonants.

The *manuscript* is theopneustic, not the *man*. The inspiration of the Vowel-points—part of that manuscript—is therefore seen to be integral, vital. Of course, if the *pen-strokes* are inspired upon the parchment, the *words* are. Give the pen-strokes, and you give the words. The establishment of the Points will, therefore, always be the establishment of the Church doctrine of exact, direct, chirographical inspiration; and not only this, but also the establishment of one straight, permanent, received, and changeless text; and this Dr. Ginsburg, himself the foremost laborer against that text, as equally against the vowel-points, most readily admits.

The constant, uniform tradition of the Jews, affirming that the points came down from Moses, and the giving of the Law, was a tradition unbroken down to the year 1538, twenty-one years after Luther had nailed up his Theses. The points were then denied by Elias Levita, a rationalistic Jew, who stood alone against the sentiment of his whole nation, at the time of writing his book.* "It is to the Massoreth Ha Massoreth of Levita," as Dr. Ginsburg admits, "that we owe the present modern controversy concerning the antiquity and inspiration of the Points." "The rejection of the Points," as he admits, "by men of laxer tendency, following Levita, produced most lamentable effects, especially so far as the criticism of the Old Testament is concerned"†—effects, indeed, we may add, from which we have not yet recovered, but which, in spite of all the resistance of a sound and a loyal conservatism, are still seen working themselves out in the popular, so-called, "Higher Criticism" of the day. "It was," continues Dr. Ginsburg, "the unwarrantable liberty taken with the text, first started by Capellus, following in the wake of Levita, and the resort to all sorts of emendations and conjectural readings, in order to sustain the peculiar and the preconceived fancies of different individuals and schools, which converted the controversy about the Vowel-points into an Article of Faith in the Reformed Church of Switzerland, and led to the enacting of a law in 1678 that no person should be licensed to preach the Gospel in the churches, unless he publicly declared that he believes in the integrity of the Hebrew text, and in the Divinity of the very Vowel-points."

The last Doctrinal Confession of the Reformed Church

---

*Buxtorf, Tractatus de Punc, Origine. Caput II, p. 3.
†Massoreth Ha Massoreth, p. 61.

of Switzerland, the *Formula Consensus* of 1675, drawn up by Heidegger and Turrettin, and which fitly closes the period of the great Calvinistic confessions, says as follows:

"In particular, do we accept the Hebrew Codex of the Old Testament, which comes to us from the hands of the Jewish Church, to which were formerly committed the 'Oracles of God'; and we firmly maintain it, not only as to the consonants, but also as to the vowels, *sive ipsa puncta,* the very points; the words as well as the things, as *theopneustos*—God-breathed—part of our faith, not only, but our very life."

The question is settled for us, however, not by traditions or confessions, but by the Book itself.

THE BIBLE TESTIFIES THE INSPIRATION OF THE POINTS

1. It says, with reference to the Tables of the Law, that they were the work of God absolutely; and that the writing was the writing of God—the whole of it; and that it was graven of God—every scratch of it. See Exod. xxxii. 16.

2. Our Saviour tells us that part of these scratches were "jots," or *yodhs,* and "tittles," or little pointed marks, and that not one of these shall pass away. The words of Christ, "jot," "tittle" (see Matt. v:18), are no repetition of some common and exaggerated proverb, and they are no tautology. They mean, in all Divine intention and *emphasis,* just what they say, and they refer to the specimen of the two Tables, not only, but to the whole scope of Scripture as well. "Seeing our Saviour," says Fulke—the great champion of Protestantism—"seeing our Saviour hath promised that never a prick (*i. e.,* a vowel point) of the Law shall perish, we may understand His words of all the prophets, for we do not receive the vowels from some later Jews, but from the Prophets themselves." Such, also, is the comment of the distinguished Hebraist, Hugh Broughton, as well as that of the great Piscator, (who says: "It appears from this text (Matt. v:18), that the Holy Bible, in the time Christ, had the points, and that these points were confirmed by our Saviour."

3. The Bible asserts the inspiration of the very vowel-points, because it says, "Words which the Holy Ghost

teacheth"—the *words*. "Words," notice, not *"half-*words" —not wind-swept skeletons, which wait to be filled in by human conjecture. Consonants are not words, and if men can make vowels, they can also make consonants, and so make their own words, and so make a Bible. Nor does the minuteness of the vowel-point impugn the argument, since God, who can engrave an Aleph, can equally engrave a Kibbuts or a Sheva. Exod. xxxii:16, says that He did so.

4. The inference is unavoidable from Deut. xxvii:8, where the command is given to write "very plainly"— literally to cut each mark in deep. This must include the vowel-marks, as well as consonants, for on them, most of all, the plainness must depend. There are innumerable passages where, without the vowel-points, no man alive can tell the meaning of the Holy Ghost, nor know the mind of God.

Rome opposes, with all her most virulent force, the vowel-points, because, once rid of *these,* she makes the Church the arbiter—the umpire and interpreter. The Church puts in the points.

This anti-scriptural and arrogant assumption of exclusive rights in the monopoly of truth—the very doctrine of the scribes and Pharisees who sit in Moses' seat—was never voiced more boldly than by that bulwark of the papacy. Morinus, who does not hesitate to put it that "the reason why God ordained the Scriptures to be written in this ambiguous manner (*i. e.,* without the Points), is because it is His will that every man should be subject to the judgment of the Church, and not to interpret the Bible in his own way. For seeing that the reading of the Bible is so difficult, and so liable to various ambiguities, from the very nature of the thing, it is plain that it is not the will of God that every one should rashly and irreverently take upon himself to explain it; nor to suffer the common people to expound it at their pleasure; but that in those things, as in other matters respecting religion, it is His will that the people should depend upon the priests."

Counter to this entire principle of Rome, Protestantism stands for the points, and the more, that she is driven to substitute for an Infallible Church, an Infallible SOMETHING—a Bible.

"The Bible," says Protestantism, "is independent of all men—of all tradition, of all councils, of all decretals and canons. It needs no Pope; nor college of scarlet-frocked cardinals; no Ecumenical Assembly to endorse its claim."

"The Church," says Protestantism, "is built on the Bible, and not the Bible on the Church." The Church is to be shaped to the Bible, not the Bible to the Church. The Church is to return to the Bible, not the Bible to the Church. The Church is not the keeper of the Bible, but the Bible keeps the Church. The only barrier against backsliding; the only hope in reform; the only power to heal, that is vital, is the Book of Books, and the conviction that its every utterance and every pen-stroke is Divine.

5. A fifth and final indirect but powerful testimony of the Scripture to the vowel-points, is in the marginal notes which the Hebrew brings with it—the so-called *Keri Ve-Kethib*. The Keri in the margin nowhere changes the *vowels* of the text. The margin everywhere testifies to the vowel-points as authentic. *It is the consonants in every instance that are changed.*

The Vowel-points then, according to the Scripture as well as the universal Jewish tradition, are an integral part of the text—of the very handwriting of God. The Kabbalah (Sohar I; 15, b.) asserts that "the Vowel-points proceeded from the same Holy Spirit who indited all the sacred Scriptures."

Suppose one to take the opposite ground, that the consonants alone were inspired and the vowels, a human invention, were afterward introduced. Now see the difficulties:

When? At what moment were they introduced? Such a change as the pointing over—from Genesis to Malachi—of an unpointed Bible must have produced among Christians, as well as Jews, little less than an earthquake.

Press the argument further: The Points are in existence. They are here. Not only do we have books written and printed *without* them, but we have books WITH them, the Great Temple Copy, of which these shorthand, ephemeral copies are briefs. *Where did the points come from which are to-day upon the MSS. considered as authority?* Those MSS. which regulate criticism and are the unswerving conservators of the true text? The points upon those MSS, whence did they come?

Press the argument still further. It is said that the points were invented by the Masorites because we get them from the Masorites, but the question echoes and still echoes, "Whence did they get them?" Press the argument home to the wall. It is said that the points were *invented* by the Masorites. It is said so, because Levita first said so. But what did he know about it? Nothing. He stood, as Buxtorf shows, alone—a single man against the sentiment and history of his whole nation. His speculation was built rashly up on a conjecture like a blind man's dream— upon a fancy, rootless as a mushroom growth. There were several schools of the Masorites. Which school invented the points? Why did not other schools—the jealousy of scholars is proverbial—observe, dissent, dispute them? How explain the miracle of a complete unanimity and unexceptional subjection to the school of Tiberias, if school of Tiberias it was? How account for it that childish, doting Rabbins of Tiberias, "men more mad than Pharisees, bewitching with traditions and bewitched, blind, crafty, raging," should have shown such nice Divine composure and exactness as appears in all the adaptations of the points? "Look at the men," says Dr. Lightfoot in his masterly response to Walton's Prolegomenon. "Read over the Jerusalem Talmud, and see there how R. Judah, R. Chaninah, R. Hoshaia, R. Chija Rabba and the rest of the grand Masorites behave themselves. How earnestly they labor at nothing; how childishly they handle serious disputes, how much froth, venom, smoke—pure nothing in their disputations. Then if you can believe the pointing of the Bible came from such a school," become a Jew yourself, "believe also their Talmuds. The pointing of the Bible savors of the work of God the Holy Ghost and not of that of lost and blinded and besotted men."

Allowing the question to be narrowed down to the Masorites, let us consider a little more closely who or what were these men who by the merest freak of conjecture are supposed to be the authors of so great a work as giving vowels to the lifeless consonants that stood for Hebrew words.

1. Admitting that there was, at any time, at Tiberias, or anywhere else, a body of Jews having in hand the fixing of the Divine text in a permanent form—then confessedly those Jews would be men to whom the Word of God had never been committed as a trust, as it had been to their fathers before their rejection: men who had no interest in or title to it or right to deal with it. Castaways from the Covenant they were; whose "house had been left to them desolate." Men blinded they were, without the Holy Ghost to guide them—with a veil upon their hearts—utterly incapable of understanding the Scriptures, the letter of which they held in their hands, or of finding Christ in them. Was God likely to give such men the power to put soul into the dead carcase of the letter? Would He inspire such men to supplement and rectify an inadequate and therefore faulty text, left to them by "the finger of God?" Would He teach them to invent and add what prophets and apostles had been ignorant of from the foundation of the world?

2. These Masorites, whoever they were, were men so far from fit to interpret the mind of God in the Scriptures or even to approximate a knowledge of the truth, that they were desperately engaged in opposing and denying the claims of Christ in the Gospel to their own confusion and final destruction. Their business was the turning of the truth of God into a lie; how then could they do aught to preserve it?

3. The Masoretic theory of the origin of the points is contradicted by the very points themselves. The gloss upon Isa. 53 which, in order to get rid of a suffering Messiah had been put upon it, by the Chaldee paraphrast, and in which the sufferings, instead of being *endured* by Christ, were represented as *inflicted by Him on His enemies*—this gloss, of centuries before, was well known and accepted by these Rabbins of Tiberias, why then, if they put in the points, did they not point the text to correspond with their interpretation? Surely they would have done this, had they had control of the pointing. They did not do it because the points were already there 2000 years before their day and

though the points were against them they did not dare to change them—nor could they change them had they dared.

4. These Tiberian rabbins, the Masorites, were men under the special curse of God—His vengeance on account of the shedding of the Blood of His own dear Son. To no such men did God commit the integrity of the "Lively Oracles." As well commit it to the hands of Satan himself.

5. These Masorites were men of the densest ignorance as to anything outside their traditions—as appears from such stories as that in which they make Phyrrhus King of Epirus in Greece help Nebuchadnezzar against Jerusalem and other like nonsense.

Of all the foolish fables ever invented, this is the most absurd and incredible, that obscure and ignorant men of Tiberias—men about whom we know nothing—men the creations of credulity itself—phantoms like the false Dream sent to Agamemnon,—in a time of grossest ignorance, and living among a people abandoned to error and themselves blinded under the curse of God, should—without any consultation with Babylonian or any Jewish schools—all at once find out and carry to perfection a work so great, so excellent, so incomparable, so transcendent as the fixing for all time of a Divine authoritative text which had hitherto been fluctuating and mutable—that they should do this, and that the whole world, Jewish and Christian, without a single demurrer or dissenting voice, should receive it, implies a miracle so portentous, so impossible, so self-contradicting, that to believe it requires one to empty his brains out. Were I convinced that the pointing of my Hebrew Bible depended upon such men as the Masorites, I would shut it up in despair of ever knowing its contents. "He who reads without the points," says Rabbi Isaac, "is like a man who rides a horse $\dot{a}\chi\acute{a}\lambda\iota\nu o\varsigma$ without a bridle, to be carried whither he knows not."*

Without the vowel-points as Whitfield has suggested it is impossible to distinguish different words written with the same consonants. Take the word אֶרְחָמְךָ, Ps. 18:1, which by a change in the vowels and

*See along this line of argument, Owen on the Vindication of the Hebrew Text.

daghesh, may be read in 125 different ways. Take again the case of the conjugation of the verb, in which the Kal, Piel and Pual are, so far as the consonants are concerned, precisely alike and are to be distinguished only by the vowel-points. The Kal and the Piel are *active*; the Pual is *passive*. The word קטל without the points is either "he killed," or "he was killed" with no way to determine which. In the future tenses it would be even worse; for example in the word פקד, where the Kal, the Niphal, the Piel, the Pual, the Hiphil and the Hophal without the vowels are the same. So that six out of the seven conjugations of the verb without the vowels are precisely alike. Thus the copiousness, variety and exquisite accuracy claimed for the shades of meaning in the Hebrew verb are gone and there remains only perplexity and confusion.

Another argument for the antiquity and inspiration of the points may be drawn from the irregularities in form and grammar which occur, and which would never have been left in the text had Masorites or any other human experts had the pointing of the text. Take one example which must suffice for all. Had the vowels been put in by the Masorites, they would never, with their technical and finical regard for the small points of grammar, have left Daniel to address King Belshazzar in the *feminine* instead of the masculine form. Daniel probably addressed the effeminate king in that way—surrounded as he was by women and perhaps, like Sardanapalus, more or less dressed like one and posing like one in his dissolute feast—in order to suggest his shame as well as guilt while he pronounced his terrible and petrifying doom.

Vowels are the life of a language. They are to the consonants what the soul is to the body. It is significant that a vowel begins and a vowel ends the Greek alphabet taking in all the letters between them. Nor is it less significant that Christ, the Eternal Word, exclaims: "I am the vowels: I am Alpha and Omega, the beginning and the ending, the first and the last—I speak everything."

Vowels are the life of a language—the consonants are not. The consonants are simply stops upon the breath; but the breath—Ah, E, O,—Ye, Ho, Vah—is primal, the soul. As says the Kabbalah the oldest and most eminent

Jewish authority, "Consonants are the body and the vowel-points the soul; the consonants move with the motion and stand still with the resting of the vowel-points just as an army moves after its sovereign." "Vowels," says Dr. Gill, "are the life and soul of language. Letters without them are indeed *dead* letters; the consonants stubborn immovable things; they cannot even be pronounced without vowels which are, as Plato says, 'their necessary bond.'" That therefore, the Hebrew, the first and most perfect of all, God's own peculiar language, should be without them, is inconceivable.

No written language can be read without the vowels. I once went down into the Hebrew quarter of New York City to convince myself of this. It is easy enough to read an unpointed text when one knows the pointed text thoroughly, as readers in the synagogues who are instructed can do. But to seize the exact word and sense without the vowels is impossible, and to teach little children and beginners in a language, without them, is impossible. Even our simple English could not be taught to little children by the consonants alone. Three consonants can stand for at least a dozen words; four can stand for more than fifty. Think of the strain upon the memory. Think of the nice exercise of judgment in taking in the scope of the connection. Think of the fine instinct necessary to discern the intention of the writer and so to choose the vowels that exactly make the words that reproduce his thought; and then imagine that the complicated Hebrew could be preserved and taught and understood; and *God's* thought,—no merely human thought—perfectly transmitted, by jangling consonants without connecting links—*Credat Judaeus Apella!*

To all these arguments may again be added the care of the Jews in copying. The original manuscript written by Moses himself, must, in the course of time, have perished—although that "Book of the Law" (see 2 Kings xxii:8), seems yet to have existed in King Josiah's day. Copies therefore, would be called for at a very early date. Accordingly we find rules of the severest stringency laid down for the copyist. The Temple Manuscript ruled Supreme. When a manuscript showed traces of age and of use, it was burned with the extremest care and solemnity. Before this it was copied by official scribes,

THE DOCTRINES OF GRACE

These scribes were to write with a specially prepared black ink upon a new parchment from the hide of a clean animal. Every skin must contain a certain number of columns of prescribed length and breadth. The number of lines must be the same in each column; the number of words the same in each line. No word must be written till the copyist has first inspected it in the example before him and pronounced it aloud. Before writing the name of God he must wash his pen. All redundancy or defect of letters must be scrupulously avoided. Prose must not be written as verse, nor verse as prose; and when the copy has been completed it remains for examination and approval or rejection thirty days. From all this who can fail to be persuaded of the accurate transmission of the very "jots" and "tittles" of the law?

"But the synagogue copies have been and are unpointed. Why?"

One reason, perhaps, was and is the labor saved in copying. The same consideration leads *us* in writing to employ abbreviations.

A reason more serious was that of the Cabalists and other allegorizers, who wished to make the Word of God confirm their comments and traditions; that they might give their own interpretation to the text. "When the letters are not pointed," says R. Menachem, "they have many faces (or interpretations), but when they are pointed they have only one sense according to the punctuation." The unpointed text allowed the rabbins opportunity for free thought, which opportunity they embraced, "making the Word of God of none effect through their traditions." In sympathy with this same spirit human nature loves to monopolize whatever good may be and the more valuable the good, the more exclusive and determined the monopoly. Nor are hierarchies by any means an exception. The rabbins then and learned men would favor an unpointed text which gave them scope for the assumption of authority in deciding what was the text and what must be its meaning. This secured great honor, influence and power for the clergy, while the common people were deprived of a plain text from which they could draw their own conclusions, and which they could make their independent guide. These are the men who "sat in Moses' seat," against whom our Lord so severely inveighs when He says: "Woe unto you Scribes and Pharisees, hypocrites, for ye shut up the kingdom of heaven against men, for ye neither go in yourselves, neither suffer ye them that are entering to go in. Woe unto you lawyers, for ye have taken away the *key* of knowledge. Ye entered not in yourselves, and them that were entering in ye hindered."

In perfect accord with this spirit, we have Rome's vehement defence of the Masoretic pointing of the Hebrew text. As soon as the notion of the late invention of the points was broached by Elias Levita, the Church of Rome embraced and endorsed it as an argument for the uncertainty and unreliability of the Old Testament text; the necessary consequence of which uncertainty must be the setting up of the Church in place of the Scripture, as the infallible authority, and Arbiter of truth. "Scripture," says Rome, "has no authority but what it receives from the Church." Joannes Morinus, in his preface to an edition of the Septuagint printed at Paris, A. D. 1628, does not hesitate to state this proposition in the plainest words: "The doctrine of salvation is by Divine Institution made," he says, "to depend upon the authority of the Church. A remarkable evidence whereof, amongst others, is *the perpetual uncertainty and ambiguity of the Hebrew text by reason of the absence of the points.*" Dr. John Owen, defending the inspiration of the points and speaking of Morinus, says, "He makes the Hebrew tongue to be a very *nose of wax* to be turned by men which way they please and so to be given of God on purpose that men might subject their consciences to an infallible church. In nothing do they, the Papists, so pride themselves as in the conceit of the novelty of the Hebrew punctuation, whereby they hope with Abimelech's servants, utterly to stop the wells and fountains from which we should draw our soul's refreshment." If the Hebrew points are not an original part of the text, and if they were not *ab origine,* before ever a Masorite was born, then the text is indeed uncertain nor can any man be instructed, reformed, confirmed or established by an uncertainty. If the points are not authentic they are of no value and we, as honest men, can have nothing to do with them.

If the points were put in by the Masorites on a tradition

THE DOCTRINES OF GRACE

of sounds afloat in the air for thousands of years, it was done by a miracle. It was indeed, considering who these Masorites were, *Satan inspired to make scripture!*

Moreover: it is as easy to believe that the *consonants* came floating down in the air by tradition and that *their* characters were invented as to believe this of the points. "But," one says, "the consonants existed, they are here!" So did the points exist, they are equally here. "But Jerome who finished the Vulgate translation of the scriptures in the year 420 says nothing about the points!" No, and neither do we, in translating, say anything about them. We take them for granted and so did he. Else why—for example, does he say "You must not read זכר, you must be sure to **read** זכר? What nonsense! If there were no points to distinguish the words it would be the same as saying in English, "You must not read B L K "black," you must read B L K "block," or "balk" or "bleak" or "bloke," or what not. Jerome had the points as his entire translation proves.

The Hebrew text, as we have it, came down unchanged from Moses. This is clear, not only from the fact that the men who deny the antiquity of the points differ among themselves as to when and by whom the points were put in —whether in the year A. D. 500 or 800; whether by later or by earlier Masorites, or by Ezra or by some one else they know not whom. The only thing they agree in is the denial of the points as Divine. To us they are Divine or nothing. The most simple, perfect, beautiful, exquisitely self consistent system of punctuation ever known to man was not the invention of any darkened brain of doting Masorite; nor was it the invention of the brighter brain of either Ezra or Moses. God shines through the "jots" and "tittles" of His law as gloriously as through the stately, square and upright characters which—like Heaven's windows, open out eternal lights and grandly represent the most majestic language in the world.

And yet again an argument—why do the points exist at all? Because they are needed. Nothing not needed survives. But, if needed now they have been needed from the beginning—each "jot" and each "tittle," why not?

No one ever doubted the authenticity of the points until Levita, a rationalistic Jew, surprised his nation with his

Massoreth Ha Massoreth. Ludovicus Cappellus, a Protestant professor in Saumur—a man unsound in his theology, whose sympathies were with the Church of Rome, of which, his son who aided him was a bigoted member—followed up Levita's line of argument. The whole scheme—exposed and confuted by Buxtorf in his *Tiberias,* and condemned by the orthodoxy of the Reformed Church—leaves the points to-day as indelible upon the manuscript as when they were put there by the finger of God. If any scripture is inspired they are.

Nor is it to any purpose whatsoever that men contend that the points are too numerous and too minute to claim the thought and finger of Almighty God. He, to whom the wonders of the microscope are as infinite as those of astronomy: He who does not disdain to count the hairs of our head; to fix a thousand fascets in the eye of an insect, or to guide the circulation of a million animalcules in a drop of water, can make and count and fix vowel-points as easily as He can make volcanoes, or fix the number of the constellated and unconstellated stars. If He has magnified His Word above all His name, i. e., above all His other manifestations, then He has magnified it in the minute as well as in the magnificent—in the "jots" and "tittles" as well as in the hewing of the tables of the law. In bringing forward this argument our opponents therefore, "like Goliath, carry a sword which cuts off their own heads."

The entire contention, as to the points comes to this: Is the Bible the Infallible Rule and Ultimate Appeal in religion, or is Tradition the Rule: or the Church of Rome the Rule: or fluctuating Opinion—what men call "consciousness"— the Rule? The contention, then, is not one of quibbles, *it is one of life and death.* The men who hold the literal inspiration of everything in scripture are safe. The men who seek to undermine or weaken that foundation will find that "the beginning of strife" with Almighty God "is as when one letteth out water." The Bible itself is lost before that strife has been ended.

The whole question of the vowel-points resolves to this. *Does God know anything about them?* Is He ignorant of the shape or the value of a Kametz or a Seghol? If not, if He knows that they are in the text, He equally knows how they came there. And as scripture everywhere, in every word is fixed by these vowels the vowels themselves must be authentic. However, placed where they are, they were placed there by God. That is all that we mean and that is just what we mean and what we stand for when we contend unflinchingly and *ad extremum* for the vowel-points as inspired.

THE HEBREW SQUARE LETTER

Men, to get rid of the vowel-points have gone further and denied the forms of the *consonants* as well. They have claimed that the square character—the most majestic, regal and superb of texts, is but an innovation upon an earlier ugly, uncouth and barbaric text styled the Samaritan.

To this, it may be replied:

1. It is not likely that the Law of God given to Shemites would first be written in the language of the accursed race of Canaan.

2. There is no hint of a change of characters, from Samaritan to square, at or before the time of the captivity. If such a change there was, it must have been known to both Nehemiah and Ezra who give us no hint of it.

3. Justin Martyr asserts that Moses, under a divine inspiration, wrote his history in *Hebrew* letters; he does not say "Samaritan letters," although he himself was a Samaritan. He also says that out of the ancient books, *written in Hebrew letters,* the Septuagint or 70 elders made their translation.

4. The Hebrew letters of the alphabet found in consecution as the headings of the verse of Ps. CXIX and elsewhere correspond, as Dr. Gill has pointed out, with the things which they signify; as א signifies an *ox*, and looks like the head and horns of one; ב signifies a *house* and looks like it; ד a *door* of which it describes the lintel and post. The Samaritan characters look like nothing and signify nothing. The Hebrew letters are the originals which give names to all others.

5. The Hebrew has five *double forms* of letters, i. e.,—one form for the middle, and another form of the same letter for the end of the word. These are found throughout the whole Bible while the Samaritan has no final letters and nothing to correspond with them.

6. The words "Holiness to the Lord" on the mitre of the high-priest were never written in Samaritan nor did any Jew ever question whether they were written in the square letter or *Hebrew*.

7. The Hebrew character is the grandest, most majestic, most expressive, most symmetrical and elegantly formed character in the world. God wrote it. It speaks its Divine origin in its frank and upright form as contrasted with all other circular and serpentine and crooked alphabetic writings. The character itself is the sublime and solemn autograph of God. Straight-forward, perpendicular, reliable, consistent, unmistakable, invariable, without the shadow of turning, it never has changed and it never will. Forever, O Lord, Thy Word is *settled* in heaven.

To all this, the unbroken and unanimous belief of the whole Hebrew nation, an objection has been brought from certain alleged Samaritan coins dug up in Judea. It is said of these coins that they were more ancient than the captivity and that the inscriptions upon them in the Samaritan characters are a proof that the Samaritan character was the character in use among the Jews before the captivity.

It is easy, in reply, to say:

1. There is no evidence whatsoever that these coins existed before the times of the Maccabees.

2. They had Greek on one side and so-called Samaritan on the other. The alleged Samaritan looks as much like Hebrew as it does like anything else. Moreover there is not one of these coins which by experts like Ottius, Reland, Spanheim and others has not been found to be spurious. Men capable of writing spurious Gospels were capable of inventing spurious coins.

3. There were plenty of coins in silver and brass with *inscriptions in the square character;* coins which dated back to Solomon and back of him to David. The Jews in the Talmud, as quoted by Dr. Gill, affirm this. R. Azariah says that he saw in Mantua a silver coin having on the one side "King Solomon," in the holy tongue and square letter, and on the other side the form of the temple. Equal testimonies have been given by Hottinger, Wagenfeil, Selden and others.

In Isa. ix:6 a final ם is found in the middle of a word.

THE DOCTRINES OF GRACE

If Isaiah was written in Samaritan, how account for that final letter which the Samaritan lacked?

Again: The letters of the word Jehovah written vertically in the square letter make the human figure and even in the dawn of Genesis, fore-shadow incarnation. Did God mean to fore-shadow it? Then He wrote in the Hebrew square letter, for the Samaritan is incapable of any such thing. That God meant something by it the Jews have always believed, for they early discovered the resemblance and called the *Tetragrammaton* a mystery. It is a mystery and stamps the Hebrew characters divine. Oh for light upon the light of the letter that in God's light we may see light!

SHEOL:
THE PRINCIPLE AND TENDENCY OF THE REVISION EXAMINED *

"'The wicked shall return to Sheol.' And in Hell he lift up his eyes, being in torments."—Ps. 9:17, Luke 16:23.

I have set before myself a simple, straightforward task—to translate into the language of the common people and in lines of clear, logical light the principles involved in the new version of the Bible and just in what direction it tends. This thing is needed. Nothing at the present moment is more needed nor so needed, for I am convinced that the principle at the root of the revision movement has not been fairly understood, not even by many of the revisers themselves, who, charmed by the siren-like voices addressed to their scholarly feeling, have yielded themselves to give way, in unconscious unanimous movement, along with the wave on which the ship of inspiration floats with easy and ac-

---

*This discourse was preached June 7, 1885, soon after the Revised Bible first appeared. It is reprinted now with later comments, simply because the principles involved remain the same and will apply to the "American" or any other similar Revision made upon the unsound basis of a change, not of the *English* only, but of the ORIGINAL GREEK ITSELF, by substituting Tischendorf's ℵ backed by the doubtful and imperfect Vatican, for the purer text of earlier and better MSS. in the possession of the Protestant and Greek Churches: and to which the Greek Church, by the imprimatur of her patriarchs unswervingly adheres. The old *textus receptus*, in spite of Westcott and Hart and their disciples, is the purest Greek text in the world. This age will invent nothing better.

And it is a significant fact that the British and Foreign Bible Society is about to replace one of its editions of the Greek Testament, now run out in Athens, by a reprint of the text of the Greek Church bearing the imprimatur of the Patriarch Constantine E. The preface of that Greek Testament says;

"This edition has aimed at, as nearly as possible, an exact reproduction of the oldest ecclesiastical text and particularly of the text of the Church of Constantinople." This Greek is that on which the authorized Version of 1611 was based, the translators being in touch with Constantinople from whence the Codex A in the British Museum came, presented as it afterward was to Charles I by Cyril Lucas, Patriarch of Constantinople.

THE DOCTRINES OF GRACE

celerating motion, toward rebound and crash upon the rocks.

Men have been talking about certain texts—they have been criticizing changes on the surface, but not one man in 10,000, certainly not one in 1,000, of the masses I mean, sees sharply to the ganglionic centre of that poison which works out so many plague-spots to the open day.

To kill the principle is to kill the whole thing; and this at last is the issue, the only point worthy of labor. The questions and the quibbles about isolated texts, headings of chapters and divisions, are comparatively incidental. What lies under them and determines them at last is the grand question as to the whole theory and fabric of the new higher critical system as applied to the Greek of the New Testament and reflected in its influence from that upon the Old —a system which time, as I must believe, is sure to demolish from its πρωτον ψευδος its false premise, as the first brick standing in a row, and falling on its neighbor, prostrates all the rest.

That a few changes might be made in both Testaments, for the better, no man pretends to deny; but that all the learned twaddle about "intrinsic and transcriptional probability," "conflation," "neutral texts," "the unique position of B," the Vatican manuscript, and behind it the "primitive archetype," *i. e.*, text to be conjectured, not now in existence; and finally the flat and bold and bad assertion that "we are obliged to come to the individual mind at last,"—that all this so-called science shutting right up to one "group" of manuscripts, at the head of which are two—both of them, ℵ and B, as the drift of the proof goes to show, of a common, perhaps questionable, Egyptian, origin—one of them discovered in 1859, and first published in October, 1862, *little more than twenty years ago*—the other the Vatican Codex, supposed to be earlier, first—and behind that forsooth, to supply its defects, conjecture, cloudland, where divine words float on the air,—that all this theory is false and moonshine and, when applied to God's word, worse than that; I firmly believe.

But *you*—suppose you believe so—why should you interest yourself? *Sauve qui peut*—why not save yourself and leave things to go as they may?

Because I am a minister of Christ, just as responsible to God as any man or minister on earth; because my business is to preach and to defend this book, and, shake this book beneath me, I am gone. "If the foundations be destroyed what can the righteous do?"

But why not speak before? Why now?

Because I have been waiting four years for other, abler men to speak; because my knowledge and my convictions have been but slowly maturing, and because there was not special reason before, such as the appearance of the whole Bible revised now suggests.

But you have already done enough in what you have said to unburden your mind; why not let the subject there stay?

Reply—We never have done enough until we have struck the last needed blow. The story of Joash and the arrows is here in point: "And Elisha said unto the king, 'Smite upon the ground.' And he smote thrice and stayed. And the man of God was wroth and said, thou shouldest have smitten five or six times; then hadst thou smitten Syria till thou hadst *consumed* it; whereas now thou shalt smite Syria but thrice."

We have never done enough until we dealt, to what we find to be error, the *coup de grace*.

A man must make it his choice either to have God upon his side or men. I am confident that if I did not say what I am about to say I should be silent from the fear of man, and I prefer to fall into the hands of God.

I know that the Revision up to this moment controls and has controlled the Reviews of this country, and has had it in its hands to make and lead opinion, as it would, the last ten years.

And yet I am persuaded that truth always carries such a terrible weight in its favor that none of its defenders need hesitate to speak. A sword in the hands of a child is mightier than a straw in the hands of a giant, and no amount of earnestness can be condemned when pleading, on straight lines, the cause of God. "To employ soft words and honeyed phrases," says Dr. Thornwell, "in discussing questions of everlasting importance; to deal with errors that strike at the foundations of all human hope as if they were harmless and venial mistakes; to bless where God disapproves, and to make apologies where He calls us to stand up like men and assert, though it may be the aptest method of securing popular applause in a sophistical age, is cruelty to man and treachery to Heaven. Those who on such subjects attach more importance to the rules of courtesy than they do to the measures of truth do not defend the citadel, but betray it into the hands of its enemies. Charity for the persons of men, whatever their opinions, is a Christian virtue, but I have yet to learn that the opinions themselves fall under its scope. On the contrary, I apprehend that love for Christ, and for the souls for whom He died, will be the exact measure of our zeal in exposing the dangers by which men's souls are ensnared."

Sentiments like these, my brethren, add their impetus to my conviction. Rather than keep silent from the fear of any consequences that may come to me, I must prefer to fall into the hands of God.

And indeed there is pressure upon me to speak. We are told in the Book, which is in the balance to-day, that "the priest's lips should keep knowledge." That does not mean "keep it in," but preserve it and translate it into plain and honest idiom, and show, in their relation, facts and principles which are at any time astir.

The fact and principle astir just now is fundamental. It is not only the question of doctrines taught by the book, but of the *book*.

And not only of the book, but of the unity of an English speaking Protestantism. The French Protestants have three different versions—those of Osterwald, Martin, Segond. In their churches and homes sometimes one is read, sometimes another. A while ago I was worshipping in a French Church in Paris. The minister read from one version, I looked over another. At the bottom of the page I find pencilled, "Not two words in five alike!" Imagine the influence of such a variation on our united front against the infidel and Rome. Study its influence upon French Protestantism in the past and now. Consider the force of the objection, "You have different Bibles and neither, or none is exact." Consider the effect upon our children to have nothing settled; to feel that Holy Scripture is a nose of wax to be twisted hither and thither. Consider the effect of all this upon what is, alas! too infrequent just now, the committing to heart of the very words of the Book as the binding dictate of God.

"Our authorized version is the one religious link which at present binds together ninety millions of English-speaking men scattered over the earth's surface." Imagine the effect of lightly loosening upon these, the power and pressure of that mighty, holy bond! Better a few archaisms, a few quaint, perhaps inadequate expressions, than such an unforeseen but logical result as that.

When it comes to the Bible, our heirloom, the charter of our personal hopes for eternity, we *all* are interested, and may well be interested, and the more that the great work in this and all divine directions has never been exclusively accomplished by men, however gifted and however honored, and most justly honored, who sit in theological chairs; but also by the help of plain pastors—of men at rough work—of men in personal contact and dealing with souls as well as the book—of men like Athanasius, Augustine and Wickliffe and Huss and Calvin and Boston and Edwards.

So that we all have an interest and are all responsible for an influence, and have all a very ample and appropriate apology for giving thought to this question.

Hitherto I have spoken of the New Testament revision and that is indeed my main point. I have shown—

I. *That it is impracticable,* unelastic, uncongenial, and from its many needless, disconcerting changes—more than 6,000 in all—a vexatious English.

II. *That it is a defective, unskillful translation;* a translation which mutilates the book by its unauthorized omissions, and which unsettles souls by its multiplied notes of discredit, a translation, too, which lacks those marks of spiritual apprehension and of feeling which are the supremest quality—so patent and so glowing in what we have now.

The principle of translation adopted by the Revisionists, viz.: to render the same Greek word by precisely the same English word, in each case, was false and mistaken—a principle which cannot possibly be carried out and has arrayed against it all philosophy as well. In contrast to this narrow, unadaptable, pedantic notion the old Translators, recognizing the shades of meanings in words and the place, just there, where tact and knowledge and spiritual discernment and taste must come in, laid down another and far

THE DOCTRINES OF GRACE

more scholarly principle—"We have been especially careful," they say, "and have even made a conscience, not to vary from the sense of that which we had translated before, *if* the word signified the same thing in both places, but *there be some words that be not of the same sense everywhere.*"

Principle how broad, my Brethren, how judicious! For we must remember that to translate is not to construe. Take the first line of Virgil's Eneid—*Arma virumque cano, Trojae qui primus ab oris.* A school boy tones it off and quite correctly, "Arms, man and I sing—of Troy who first from shores." That is exact, if exact means identical, but it is not a translation. Virgil is poetry. There is no poetry in the school boy's literal words. Virgil gives you a picture—the school boy gives you no picture. Virgil opens with a grand idea—the school boy gives you *no* idea, but only words.

To translate then is not simply to know a language and construe it literally. A translator must have the *Geist,* as the Germans say, of a language; the *soul;* and more, must be one with the spirit that breathes the great original words.

This men forget now-a-days. The reformers made everything of it. A natural man, they maintained, cannot perceive the things of the Spirit of God, nor can a mere scholar. Spirituality is the supremest requisite. Whatever else a man is, or is *not,* he must be spiritual to translate the things of the Spirit.

Just this explains the secret of the German Bible. Luther's translation, considering the time, the books, the helps he had, is almost supernatural. I am prepared to believe that in some true sense it was. "His choice of words in rendering the Hebrew," says Dr. Gottleib, a learned Jewish scholar, "shows a kind of inspiration." "Luther guessed at meanings which have only in later years been found the true ones." Heine says of Luther, "He translated the Bible from a language which had ceased to exist into one which had not yet arrived. Our dear Master's thoughts had not only wings but hands; his faults have been more useful to us than the virtues of a better man. How Luther got the language into which he translated the Bible is to this hour incomprehensible." Mendelssohn says of Luther, *"Wo er schlecht übersetzt hat, hat er doch vortrefflich verdeutscht."*

Where, in translating, he has blundered he has made inimitable German.

But Luther's blunders are next to infinitessimal and so are those of our ancient translators. Their English is mahogany, takes a polish, and bears rubbing, in comparison with which the English of the present day, *for such a purpose,* is both bass and pine-wood.

III. That the revised New Testament is based upon a new, uncalled for, and unsound Greek text—that mainly of Drs. Westcott and Hort, which was printed simultaneously with the revision and never before had seen light, and which is the most unreliable text perhaps ever printed —one English critic says, "the foulest and most vicious in existence."*

Drs. Westcott and Hort's New Testament comes to us bound in two volumes. The second volume an apology and introduction. I intend to follow that second volume straight through and make its consecutive points. I cannot give you 324 pages, but I can give you the analysis—the heads—and you can go and get the book and verify them for yourselves.†

The points are these.

I. Out of all available manuscripts, say 1,100, ℵ (the Siniatic) and B (the Vatican) stand far above the rest.

II. B the Vatican stands, for authority, far above ℵ — is older than ℵ.

III. ℵ and B, or rather B ℵ, stand for some earlier

---

*Since then we have another newer text, that of Nestle and Weidner based again on Tischendorf and incorporating the defects of Westcott and Hort; bracketing as it does Mark 16:9-20, and actually discarding John 8:1-12. The margins of my own copy of this Testament of Nestle & Weidner are blackened with the pencilled words "omission," "great omission"—"omission of 7 words"— "omission of 9 words"-"omission of 4 words"—"omission of 3 words"—"uncalled for transposition"—"change of statement by change of verbal form," &c., &c. What may be said of Westcott & Hort applies therefore to Nestle & Weidner—the principle and spirit are the same.

†Published by Harper & Bros., 1882, and marked**

THE DOCTRINES OF GRACE

manuscript not now in existence, perhaps an actual autograph.

IV. B is the nearest, earliest link with that actual autograph.

V. Since B is full of omissions—leaving out as it does I. and II. Timothy—Titus—Philemon—Hebrews from chapter IX. on, and the whole of Revelation, besides multitudes of minor omissions—2,877 words in all—we are forced back, to supply such omissions, finally, to "Conjectural emendation," "Critical instinct"—the individual mind at last.

Now I will prove my own words and make each of these points.

I. "ℵ and B stand far above all other manuscripts." Introd. page 210.

"They were written, in parts, by the hand of the same scribe." Introd. page 213.

"They were written in the same generation and probably in the same place." Page 214.

"They are no less excellent when taken all alone without the other manuscripts than when supported by them." Page 219.

"What makes them so superior is their *internal* evidence—that of which only a critic can judge." Page 219.

"They must be accepted until this internal evidence be found untrue." Page 225.

"They never can be safely rejected." Page 225.

II. As ℵ and B stand far above all others, so B stands far above ℵ—is older than ℵ Page 210, §285.

Trains of manuscripts where B leads off without ℵ are equally good with those which have ℵ, *i. e.*, B plus is equally good with ℵ, B plus. Pages 227, 238.

This is not so with trains in which ℵ leads off, *i. e.*, ℵ plus is not equal to ℵ B plus. Page 229.

The peculiar readings of B, found nowhere else, do commend themselves on their own merits. Pages 230-238 §317.

III. B and ℵ start from an earlier archetype—some lost autograph manuscript not in existence. Now let me quote verbally page 247, 248: "The ancestries of both manuscripts having started from a common source not much later than the autographs, justifies a strong initial presumption that the text of their archetype is preserved in *one or other* of them."

Again, page 287: "Whatever may be the ambiguity of the evidence in particular passages the general course of future criticism must be shaped by the happy circumstance that the fourth century has bequeathed to us two manuscripts, of which even the less incorrupt must have been of exceptional purity—which manuscripts rise into greater pre-eminence the better the early history of the text becomes known."

IV. B is earlier and much superior to ℵ, and indeed is separated from the original autograph of the Apostles by very few links—pages 248, 249—"by very few links, indeed."

This is proved:

1st. "By the fact that B is an Uncial"—is written in capital letters.

2d. "It is proved by tradition."

3d. "It is proved by the omissions in B"—criticism is the art of getting down to the bone. Whatever manuscript adds anything B does not. "The manuscript which omits most is the purest, because less clogged with extraneous matter." Page 235.

"It is on the whole safer for the present to allow for a proneness on the part of the scribe of B to *drop petty words* not required by the sense." Page 236.

That is the whole argument on which is founded the new, higher critical system.

ℵ and B are above all the others. B is above ℵ.

B with its omissions is nearest to the first and simon-pure autograph.

Where omissions are to be supplied in B the door is open for "conjectural emendation"—"personal discernment here would seem to be the surest ground." Personal instincts will be trustworthy in the degree of education and of critical experience. Quotations from pages 65, 71.

NOW, AGAINST THIS WHOLE THEORY, SIMPLE AS IT IS AND PLAUSIBLE, WHICH PLACES "B" FIRST, FOREMOST AND INFALLIBLE ARBITER, I HAVE TO REPLY.

THE DOCTRINES OF GRACE

I will oppose B the Vatican MS. first, foremost, altogether, simply *because it is the Vatican MS.*, because I have to receive it from Rome, because I will have no Bible from Rome, no help from Rome and no complicity with Rome; because I believe Rome to be an apostate. A worshipper of Bread for God; a remover of the sovereign mediatorship of Christ; a destroyer of the true gospel, she teaches a system which, if any man believes or follows *as she teaches it*, he will infallibly be lost—he *must be*.

Notice what is omitted in the Vatican MS.—*Timothy* and *Titus,* Imputation see verse 18. *Hebrews,* The doctrine of the Blood-Atonement once for all. The *Apocalypse,* Christ coming to catch up the true Church and to deal with the Mother of Harlots.

On any ground I will not pin my faith on Rome. I do not know what she has got. No man knows how many omissions she herself has made in what she has got. I will not take my Bible—not the *bulk* of it—from her apostate, foul, deceitful, cruel hands. *"Timeo Danaos et dona ferentes"*—I fear the Latins bearing presents in their hands.

And with good reason for:

1st. As to B's being an Uncial, so are four others—so are the two English MSS., A and D.

As for A (British Museum) on Drs. Westcott and Hort's own testimony, it "stands in broad contrast to both ℵ and B." And "it stands quite alone *in some manifestly right readings.*" It is probably the oldest as it is the most reliable having been in the hands of the Greek Church from time immemorial and is the base of the New Testament authorized by the Greek Church—the purest text of all.

As for D (Cambridge), the same self-betrayers admit that "the text of D presents a truer image of the form in which the Gospels and the Acts were most widely read in the third and probably a great part of the second century than any other extant Greek MS." Introd, p. 149.*

Here, then, are the two great English Uncials, both of which are undoubtely older, one of which A is in contrast

---

*The five great ℵ Uncials are A, B, C, D and . C, in Paris, is a palimpsest.

to ℵ and B, and is alone in some manifestly right readings; the other of which, D, takes us back to the best form of the text in the second century, *i. e.*, two centuries before the earliest pretensions made for the Vatican,† and that they admit. But more than this, the Cursives, *i. e.*, MSS. written in small running characters are original sources, as well as the Uncials. No MSS. are autographs. These cursive copies represent originals. Why not? No reason why not. Everybody admits that a cursive may be even, in some cases, a better authority than any uncial. Why not? The foundation of the received text of the Apocalypse was a cursive marked I.

This is strenuously insisted upon in the Preface to the Greek Testament issued under the ΣΦΡΑΠΣ, the Seal of Constantine E Patriarch of Constantinople, in 1904.

That Preface says: "This edition purposes as its end the reproduction of the most ancient text according to the Ecclesiastical tradition and especially as handed down by the Church of Constantinople. Having such an end in view, the book is prepared, not upon the basis of any printed editions whatsoever, nor upon the basis of critical editions which have made use of the Great Codices written in capital letters, but upon the basis of those copies which are commonly neglected and, to make use of a Scriptural expression, "disallowed of the builders;"—upon the basis of the Byzantine copies many of which are written in small letters and letters calling for minute inspection." Translation from the Preface to the Testament of the Greek Church the text of which agrees in every point with that of our received and authorized version. Why, when men are so valorously

---

†Professor Hug labored to prove that the Vatican was written in the early part of the 4th century, but Bishop Marsh puts it two centuries later. Horne's Introduction, Part I, Chap III. Probably both A and D are older than B and unspeakably purer. D was found by Beza in the Monastery of St. Irenæus at Lyons and represents a Western—possibly an Albigensian (Protestant) Genealogy: Greek on the left hand page and Latin on the right, the Latin translation is older than that of Jerome. Dr. Scrivener says: "It may well have been brought into Gaul by Irenæus and his Asiatic companions A. D. 170." It contains without a break Mark 16:9-15 and John 8-12 passages discounted by the Revision.—See Scrivener's Codex Bez as Cantabrigiensis Intr. ix., p. xlv. See also Horne, Pt. I., Ch. III., Sec. II., §4.

THE DOCTRINES OF GRACE

contending for the Supreme authority of the Vatican MS, does it not occur to some "critic" that it would be well to go back to the Greek Church for MSS as well as to Rome?

Just so a Version or ancient translation may be a source. The versions, it is admitted by critics, have been "too much neglected."

And once more the Fathers. Suppose St. Augustine quotes Mark ix:44, 46, 48, just as we have them: "Where their worm dieth not and the fire is not quenched." That shows that in his day at least the three-fold statement was regarded as the Word of God.

B then cannot be Emperor. A and D oppose it. The cursives oppose it. The Greek Church opposes it. The versions oppose it. The fathers oppose it. 1,100 documents oppose it.

But *tradition!* B is said to be older.

Well, it may be older, because less trustworthy, less used, and so not worn out.

Or it may not be older. It is first mentioned, anywhere, in 1475, sixty years after Huss and Savonarola were burned, ten years before Luther was born, not fifty before the Reformation. That is a pretty young document to claim to be lord over 1,100 documents, many of which may have been then, for all that we *know,* a thousand years old.

"Oh, but it is written in great capitals, and it has divisions into paragraphs such as documents had in Eusebius' time."

Yes, and what is there to prevent men from imitating a manuscript of Eusebius' time, and writing it large and for a purpose?

Besides, who knows anything about the Vatican manuscript? Its first collation, in 1669, by Bartolocci, now in Paris, was confessed to be imperfect, and that was published 100 years after Calvin and Luther.

The next was by another Italian, Mico, in 1725. A transcript made for Bentley, an Englishman, who wished to edit a Greek Testament. Imagine that. A Roman Catholic writes off a true and correct New Testament for a Protestant to publish.

The next information we get is in 1838. The history of this edition is "strange and obscure." It did not receive the approval of Rome, and nobody knows whether it was a true copy or not.

In 1845 Dr. Tregelles, armed with a letter from Cardinal Wiseman went to Rome with the design of seeing that manuscript. After much trouble he did see it. "Two prelates were detailed to watch him, and they would not let him open the volume without previously searching his pockets and taking away from him ink and paper. Any prolonged study of a certain passage was the signal for snatching the book hurriedly away. He made some notes upon his cuffs and finger nails."*

In 1867 Tischendorf, by permission of Cardinal Antonelli, undertook to study the Vatican Codex. He had nearly finished three Gospels when his efforts to transcribe them was discovered by a Prussian Jesuit spy. The book was immediately taken away. It was restored again, months later, by the intervention of Vercellone for a few hours. In all Tischendorf had the manuscript before him forty-two hours and only three hours at any one time, and all but a few of those hours were spent on the Gospels; and yet, he says, "I succeeded in preparing the whole New Testament for a new and reliable edition, so as to obtain every desired result."

Every desired result in forty-two hours—all but two or three of them spent on the Gospels alone.

Every desired result in three hours hurried glancing through 146 pages of an old and stained and mutilated manuscript written on very thin vellum, in faded ink, with its letters throughout large portions touched and retouched, bearing marks of a very peculiar treatment of the Epistles of St. Paul, and confessed to have received some corrections from the first and the filling up of certain *lacunae* (blank spaces) from the beginning.

That is the tatter of rags which is held up before us, between us and the sun, through the *lacunae* of which critics, forsooth, are to conjecture a spectral original reading. That is the theory and that is the apex and end of the theory—"conjectural emendation" consciousness as a test of what God has spoken—"critical instinct" "the ring

---

*"Story of the Manuscripts."

THE DOCTRINES OF GRACE

of genuineness" to borrow the phrases of Drs. Westcott and Hort—"What I like to read and confess."

But I am not done. One more point. The Vatican must be the purest because of *omissions!* We have cut things down to the bone. To criticize is to cut. Whatever manuscript adds anything, the Vatican does not. Retrenchment, not contribution, is her forte. The manuscript which *omits* most, which has least of God's word, is the best because the least clogged with extraneous matter. See Westcott and Hort Introd. page 235. Let me quote: "The nearer the document stands to the autograph the more numerous must be the omissions laid to its charge."

To all this we maintain not only denial, but assert just the opposite thing.

1. Omissions are what may be expected from Rome—Rome has had every opportunity to make the omissions—to tear off, for instance Hebrew IX to XIII—and all the omissions are straight in her line.

2. The principle laid down is nonsense. Take Israel in the captivity. The Ark was gone—Aaron's rod was gone—the Pot of Manna was gone—the Tabernacle curtains were gone. These things had been left in the path of bad progress—first the Curtains, then the pot of Manna, then Aaron's rod, then the Ark—relics of their apostasy all the way down.

History is against Drs. Westcott and Hort. The further back you go, if you go rightly, the *more you get* of any single document or ordinance given and settled of God.

But I am not done. Grant the principle, "the more numerous the omissions the purer, until you get back to the Vatican." By that time you have cut out four and a half whole books. But you have three or four more conjectural manuscripts back of the Vatican—three or four links. Cut out three or four books at each link, and what will you have left when you get back to Peter and Paul. Poor Paul! Poor old Calvinist! All the omissions but one are out of unfortunate Paul.

But I am not done. Grant the principle and you grant conjecture a source of God's word, "The Critical Consciousness"—Cloudland—God's word afloat on the air.

Against all this we oppose, and firmly and steadily, the principle of the old translators. "External, prima-facie evidence is after all the best guide." Call in all your manuscripts, all your data—uncials, cursives, versions, fathers—and *that reading carries, which brings the highest evidence, from numbers, from weight, from congruity with the rest of the Scriptures, and from the open and manifest mind of the Spirit of God.*

Again, we press it, that the principle, *Quod semper, quod ubique, quod ad omnibus,* applied to theology, must be applied to the Bible as well. *Call in all your data,* all witnesses from every side, and then the *"best supported reading" rules.* Not ℵ and B, and not B, the tattered Roman, but the best supported reading rules. The two English manuscripts will here be likely to come to the front again and the Vatican go where it was—to the rear.

IV. Now I have laid a good and solid and impregnable foundation. Ever since talking with a friend—an English clergyman—rector of St. Peter's in the East at Oxford, and a personal friend of one of the foremost opponents of the Revision, I have been confirmed in what had before been a growing conviction—that the Revision movement, dating from the finding of Tischendorf's ℵ, *unconsciously* to most, but consciously to the Unitarian—to the Messrs. Vance Smith, Robertson Smith,* etc.—liberal members of the New Testament Company, was running steadily in one direction through three points:

1st. To weaken and destroy the binding force of Inspiration in the very Words.

2d. To weaken and destroy the five Points of Grace founded on "Free Will a Slave."

3d. To weaken and destroy the old-fashioned notion of *Hell* as a place and a state of immediate, everlasting and utterly indescribable torment into which impenitent men go at once the moment they die.

---

*Prof. W. Robertson Smith, cashiered by the Free Church of Scotland was, however, a member of the Old Testament Revision Company. Dr. Geo. Vance Smith, another member, was a Unitarian. It is a significant fact that two such men should have been asked to help give us a Bible.

THE DOCTRINES OF GRACE 75

Now to prove these three points:

1st. The principle laid down by Drs. Westcott and Hort and reproduced from them since in the *Presbyterian Review,* tends straight and only to weaken and to destroy the binding force of inspiration in the very words.

Eight articles appeared in the *Presbyterian Review* from April, 1881, to April, 1885. They shook the country, and especially the Presbyterian Church. I do not now speak of the *worst* of those articles—of what was written in the name and spirit of so-called "advanced thought." I speak of what was written in faint protest by Princeton—of what, under doubtful, shifty and apologetic language, gave old Orthodoxy, as to Inspiration, *clean away.*

I say this—I said it in this pulpit two years ago—I said it at the Synod's room and was applauded for it—that when Princeton begins by refusing to call Inspiration an "influence," and by restricting it to "superintendence;" when Princeton goes on to *deny* that the Inspiration in God's Word is the first truth we embrace, and makes it the last truth; when Princeton asserts that "the Inspiration of the Scriptures is not in the first instance, a principle fundamental to the truth of the Christian religion, nor should we ever allow it to be believed that the truth of Christianity depends upon any doctrine of Inspiration whatever"; when Princeton admits that it is a "misapprehension" to suppose that Inspiration is, in its essence, "a process of verbal dictation," or control which God exercised over the very words, then we say that this revamping of the fundamental fallacies of Drs. Westcott and Hort gives Orthodoxy, as to Inspiration clean away.*

And when Princeton again, by another Professor, bristles up to vindicate the "rights of Reason;" when she asserts that in our criticism "we must treat the Bible just like any other writings," *i. e.*, "that the immediate testimony of Scripture to its own Inspiration is not independent of criticism," which means, if it means anything, that that testimony can be criticised, subjected to the "critical instinct" of Drs. Westcott and Hort; when she says that "the witness of the Spirit cannot be a common measure between minds,"

---
*Presbyterian Review, April, 1881, p. 226, 227, 232.

and that "the doctrine of Inspiration stands or falls with the results of critical investigation," then we say that in thus making "Reason" the ultimate criterion and arbiter of a Divine inspiration, Princeton, following the wake of Drs. Westcott and Hort, gives Orthodoxy, as to Inspiration, clean away.†

For, to admit that fallen, erring man can criticise a Supernatural testimony is—what is it? To put "Reason" at the bottom of faith instead of God's Word at the bottom of faith. Is?—what is it?—to make man a critic of Scripture instead of Scripture a critic of man; the sinner a judge of the law, not the object of law, which condemns him. And what is this but to give Orthodoxy, in point of Inspiration, away, and follow the line of the rationalistic wave, the New Departure, which, prophesied by Van Oosterzee twenty years ago, has swept through Scotland, floating to his death its Robertson Smith, and now has *us* on its tide.

For we hold, as fundamental, as to Inspiration the self-evidencing light that shines through *ipsissima verba* the very words—their native irradiation. Παδα γραφη Θεοπνευστος—it is the Scripture itself—the *writing*, not writer—that St. Paul says is God-breathed.

We take the ground that *on the original parchment* every word, line, point and jot and tittle was put there by God.

Every sacred writing, every word as it went down on the primeval autograph was God-breathed. You breathe your breath on a glass; it congeals. So God breathed originally, Divinely, out of Himself and through Moses, through St. Paul, as through a bending and elastic tube upon the sacred page.

And every scrap or relic of that original writing found anywhere in the world (and God in spite of men will take care of it all) will shine wherever you find it by native irradiation, by light convincing, overwhelming and complete, in glory all Divine. We do not say every "conjectural emendation" will so shine—in the transmission of God's word is no room for "conjectural emendation"—but every honest *writing* will so shine.

We take the ground, the Sun needs not a critic. When he shines, he shines the Sun—and so each word of God.

---

†*Presbyterian Review*, April, 1883, p. 343, 344, 345, 348, 351.

THE DOCTRINES OF GRACE 77

We take the open ground that a single stray leaf of God's Word found by the wayside by a pure savage—let it be the eighth chapter of John for instance—that that single stray leaf will so speak to that savage, if he can read it, that if he never heard or saw one syllable of the Bible before, that single leaf will shine all over to him, cry out "God!" and condemn him.

That is our doctrine, and *that,* the New Departure, led in by Drs. Westcott and Hort, and their principle in the Revision, weakens not only, but kills and destroys.

2. The principle of the Revision, based on the Vatican and critical instinct, and running through the New Testament weakens and tends to destroy the five points of grace which are founded on "free-will a slave."

The Doctrine of Grace which Luther taught against Rome is not that God makes men able to stand, and yet it depends on themselves after that, to fall or hold out, but the Doctrine is this—that *that* is grace alone which independently of works or merits on our part determines and changes the will, and "not only makes it able to stand, but guards against the possibility of future failure."

The doctrine founds upon the will of God. "Of His own will begat he us"—"it is not of him that willeth, nor of him that runneth, but of God that showeth mercy." In other words it founds upon free-will a slave. "Grace is the denial of the sovereignty and strength of man. In his natural condition man is completely nothing in regard to spiritual life, and the power that calls him from that condition is as independent of his concurrence as that which originally created him out of nothing and brought him into the world."*

This was the doctrine and it laid the foundation of the Spirit's work deep, deep, and deep in the prostration and the bondage of the human will. "Nothing in man," says Luther, "precedes grace, except his impotence and his rebellion."

Such a system as that founds down below all else—all faith—all will or want of will—on Jesus Christ as God.

If He is God He can do anything, meet anything—create

---

*Dr. Thornwell in his articles upon the Invalidity of Romish Baptism.

—renew the will—awake to righteousness and raise the dead.

The Revision weakens and removes the Deity of Christ in many places—I will mention five:

John III: 13—"The Son of Man which is in Heaven"—the words "which is in Heaven," living this moment as the Jehovah, are in the margin discredited and by Drs. Westcott and Hort are left out.†

Luke XXIII:42—The dying thief's address. The Revised Version bluntly reads, "And, he said, 'Jesus remember me;'" instead of "And he said unto Jesus, Lord, remember me,"—*i. e.*, it leaves out $Kv\rho\iota\epsilon$, Adonai. Jehovah—leaves out his Godhood.

Rom. IX:5—"Of whom is Christ—who is over all God blessed forever." The footnote drops out the assertion and makes it "And of whom is Christ." A full stop. Then—"He, who is God over all"—whoever He may be—"is blessed forever."

I Tim. 3-16—"Great is the mystery of godliness, God was manifest in the flesh." The Revision leaves out $\Theta\epsilon\delta s$ God, and renders it "Great is the mystery of *godliness*, He who was manifest in the flesh,"—*i. e.*, the manifested One was only *one phase*—the highest—of godliness, the precise rendering for which all the Unitarians have been contending the last 1,800 years.

(1.) In the first place, δs "He who" cannot be right because δs the pronoun, is masculine and $\mu v \delta \tau \eta \rho \iota o v$ to which it refers, is neuter.

(2.) Codex "A" of the British Museum makes it, according to all testimony of 300 years, $\Theta\epsilon o s$ Dr. Scrivener, the foremost English critic, says it is $\Theta\epsilon o s$.

(3.) Codex "C" makes it OC. with a cross mark inside the O and a line over which denotes a contraction.

(4.) "F" and "G," make it $\Theta\epsilon o s$—OC. with a line over.

(5.) All the cursives of St. Paul's Epistles—254 MSS., with the exception of two have $\Theta\epsilon o s$. These copies were produced in every part of Ancient Christendom and their testimony may be regarded as final.

---

†The American Revision retains this text, but discredits it in a foot-note.

THE DOCTRINES OF GRACE

(6.) Thirty out of thirty-two of the Lectionaries make Θεος.

(7.) More than twenty of the Greek fathers testify to Θεος.

To sum up:

One MS.—Five versions—two late fathers read ὅ "that which"—EIGHT *read* ὅ.

Six MSS—Only one Version, not one Greek father, read ὅς SEVEN read ος.

The footnote to the American Revision shows the same Unitarian tendency. It reads: "Of whom as concerning the flesh is Christ, he who is above all. God be blessed forever."

289 MSS.—Three Versions and more than twenty Greek fathers read with the present Version Θεος THREE HUNDRED AND TWELVE *read* Θεος.*

This sermon was preached June 7th, 1885. Soon after, I went to Europe where I spent nearly three weeks in studying this text I Tim. iii:16 on the great uncials "C" and "A." Through the kindness of Mr. Albert Le Faivre, Minister Plenipotentiary from France to the United States, I had the Codex "C" for one week under my hands to study the membrane with lenses and under full sunshine. The parchment was also held up by an attendant in front of the great window so that the light could fall through the palimpsest page. I have compared the THEOS of line 14 on folio 119, the one in dispute, with every other THEOS on the page and, out of the five, find it the plainest one there. All five are written with two letters—OY, OY, OC, OY, OΩ Two of the five only have the line, the mark of contraction, above. *One of the two, the plainest, is the one they deny.* Three of the five only have the hair mark in the Theta (Θ)—*one of these three is the one they deny.* To put it more plainly—the question is, Is it OC "who," or *is it* $\overline{OC}$ with a line over the two letters and a mark in the O, God? It is beyond question the latter. My eyes are as good as any man's.

Again: I have studied THEOS as it appears on Codex "A" (British Museum) with its mark in the Theta and its line

---

*For the above facts upon 1 Tim. iii:16, I am indebted to a masterly Treatise on the subject by the Dean of Chichester.

of contraction above. As the library assistant, Mr. Jeayes who held the parchment up so that the sunlight could shine through it, said: "That certainly is not an omicron and never was intended for an omicron. If an omicron, why does it have that extra mark inside?" "Oh," they say, "that is marked over." "Why do they say it? Marked over what?" Dr. Scrivener says his senses report it THEOS. "I have examined it twenty times within as many years," he declares, "and seeing (as every man must do for himself) with my own eyes, I have always felt convinced that Codex 'A' reads THEOS." That conviction of Dr. Scrivener is my conviction and on the very same grounds—a conviction so deep that *I will never yield it, nor admit as a text of my faith a Book pretending to be a Revelation from God which leaves that word out.* The Holy Ghost has written it—let no man dare touch it—Great is the mystery of godliness, GOD was manifest in the flesh.

"Oh, but it is only one word!" yes, but one word of Scripture of which it is said "Thou hast magnified Thy Word above all Thy Name!" "Only one Word!" But that word "GOD." Better the whole living church of God should perish than that that one word should perish. If any man take away from the words of the book of this prophecy God shall take away his part." Let criticism pause. The principle at stake is solemn.

Phil. II:10—"That at the name of Jesus every knee should bow." The Revision makes it *"in"* the name of Jesus every knee should bow"†—*i. e.*, just as they would bow in the name of St. Peter, the Virgin Mary or any other. We say the difference between bowing in the name of Jesus and at the name of Jesus, in the sense made here, with Christ exalted on the throne—in spite of the apparent *εν* which the old translators knew much better the force of and how to render—is the difference between making Jesus God and making him a creature—a mere man.

In the Old Testament, by uniformly changing the initial capital letter of the word "Spirit," in those passages, (e. g., Gen. vi:3), where the Holy Spirit, the third Person of the

---

†The Revision follows here the Douay, Roman Catholic, Testament.

THE DOCTRINES OF GRACE

adorable and undivided Trinity is evidently and directly referred to, and spelling the word with a small letter, the testimony of the whole Old Testament to the Divinity of God the Holy Ghost is, as Mr. Cardale has shown, greatly weakened. So too the spelling of words referring to Christ as "redeemer" (Job xix:25); "lord" (Psalm cx:1), with a small letter, derogates from his Godhood.

And weakening the Godhead of Christ the Revision weakens that which makes His Godhead needful to us and available—*the doctrine of the Bondage of the Will.* If we can deliver ourselves we do not need God in our flesh to deliver us. Free will is not then in every sense, as Luther held—a slave.

Luke II:14 betrays such a tendency. We have in the Authorized Version, "Peace on earth, good will toward men." The Revision changes this not only, but gives in the margin—"Greek, Peace on earth to men of good pleasure" —or, as the Roman vulgate has it, "to good-willing men"— *"to men who have a good will."*‡ For this, are only five manuscripts headed by the notorious Vatican. Against it are all other authorities. "Peace to good-willing men!" What the text asserts is that "God has a good will toward men." What the Revision asserts is that *"men have a good will toward God"* which is pure Arminianism. What man on earth has by nature a good will? Against it stand all the other known authorities—fifty-three to five.

Rom. VIII:6 and 7 betrays again such a tendency. "For to be carnally minded is death—because the carnal mind is enmity against God." Here the doctrine is that of total, thorough, universal depravity—carnally minded means a mind through and through carnal. But the Revision renders it "For the mind of the flesh is death—because the mind of the flesh is enmity"—*i. e.*, letting the mind run in a fleshly direction leads to death, to enmity which appreciably lightens the thought and makes another thing out of it.

In this connection I cite some passages from the Old Testament which, to me, show the same drift.

Take Job XV:16—"How much more abominable and filthy is man which drinketh inquity like water." In the Revision—"How much less (clean than the heavens) one

---
‡"To men of good will," Douay, Roman Catholic, Testament.

that is abominable and corrupt—a man that drinketh iniquity like water." Here a standard proof text for the *race-depravity* drops out. It is only *one*, a man, *any man who does such and such* things.

Take again: Jer. xvii:9—"The heart is deceitful above all things and desperately wicked, who can know it?" In the Revision—"The heart is desperately sick"—makes man the object of a weak compassion where the old translators made him guilty, an object of wrath.*

So too, Ps. 110:3—"Thy people shall be willing in the day of thy power." Subject the Hebrew to the closest scrutiny, and you cannot read with the Revision—"Thy people offer *themselves* willingly in the day of thy power." That is just what they do not do, offer themselves. The will of God makes them willing. Thy people shall be "willingnesses," *N'daboth.*—The plural noun is used to give a sense distributive and vivid. They shall have a new will—every man of them *B'yom Heleka*, in the day of thy "strength," of thy might, thy sovereign concentrated power.

The Revision not only weakens the Godhead of Christ, and it not only weakens the doctrine of the bottomless depravity and helplessness of fallen man and the enslaved condition of his will, but *it obscures the way of salvation by a simple instant act of faith on Christ.*

John iii:15. This glorious Gospel in the Gospel does not escape the sacrilegious hand. The Greek is as plain as A. B. C., "That whosoever believeth in Him should not perish but have everlasting life." In the Revision the words "Should not perish" are left out and the words *"may have"* are substituted for the positive *"have,"*—as if eternal life, after the act of faith, were in any way conditional or doubtful. It weakens the thought of an assured salvation upon the simple act of closing with Christ and trusting in Him.

Rom. v:1. The Revision reads it, "Being justified by faith *let us* have peace." The old text, which is the text authorized by the Greek Church as well, declares, ἔχομεν

---

*The Am. Rev. puts it "exceedingly corrupt," which is nothing like as strong as "desperately wicked." Gesenius translates אנש "malignant."

THE DOCTRINES OF GRACE 83

that "we *do have it.*" It is impossible for a man to believe on the Lord Jesus Christ and not be at peace with God.

To these instances might be added scores of others showing how ruthlessly the Revised Bible tampers with the text—It leaves out two whole verses Mark ix:44, 46. It leaves out the doxology of the Lord's Prayer. Matt. vi:13. It omits or by a footnote discredits nearly 200 words in the last three chapters of St. Luke, among them our Saviour's prayer for His murderers and the story of the angel strengthening Him in Gethsemane; as also His bloody sweat. It discredits twelve whole verses, the conclusion of St. Mark's Gospel (St. Mark xvi:9-20); and also other twelve whole verses—the story of the women *taken in* adultery—John viii:1-12.*

But I cannot go on with this point, time, not paucity of examples, forbids. In general only let me add, as a loyal son of the reformed theology and of the Reformers, that where any text is in dispute, the Calvinistic sense of it, being opposite to man's carnality, is probably the true one. There is not much danger that we shall, any of us, make ourselves too little—God too great—in the affair of salvation.

3. The third point that I make is the influence of Drs. Westcott and Hort's principle on the orthodox doctrine of Hell.

It is well known that "Modern Thought" has busied itself much with an assumed distinction between the words "Eternal" and "Everlasting." Nothing can be more sad than to find that the word Everlasting in the Revision has been in deference to this sceptical trifling, removed everywhere it occurs as a translation of the word $αἰώνιος$.

And is then Hell not everlasting? Does Eternal mean less? Something shorter? Were our fathers, the old Divines, Knox and Boston and Baxter and Edwards, all wrong in making the everlastingness of Hell the very fearful part of it? The offset in the infinity of its duration to the infiniteness of the Majesty against whom strikes our sin?

The fact is, the word $αἰώνιος$ is applied to Heaven as

---

*The American Revision incorporates these last but in a footnote throws discredit on the latter. Codex D, a fac-simile of which lies under my hand, contains them both without a break well as to Hell. It is the word which the Holy Ghost equally uses to emphasize the endless, unending durations of joy.

And is Heaven then not everlasting? What then is everlasting? How do eternity, God even, shrink themselves so to the shadows and measures of time. I tell you, men and brethren, the thoughtlessness, worldliness, apathy of this age needs help from no such impressions. Eternity in all its awful measures is too dim to even the most earnest and awake among us now.

The word Hell occurs twenty-two times in our New Testament. In the Revision it is left out ten times, and in every other instance has a note or change which lightens up the idea.

In the Old Testament the word Hell occurs thirty-one times. In the Revision, Sheol replaces it eighteen times. In eight places more, it is weakened by the notes "Grave," "Sheol." Only five times, and all those in Isaiah and Ezekiel, where it may be easily said "the word is figurative"—only five times out of thirty-one is Hell allowed to stand.

In our present Bible the word Hell occurs FIFTY-THREE TIMES. *In the Revision* ONLY FIVE TIMES *without note to relieve the idea.*

In Mark ix:44, 46, 48 our Saviour says three times over, "Where their worm dieth not and the fire is not quenched." The revised New Testament leaves out two whole verses—44 and 46—*i. e.*, leaves out our Saviour's words—put there as we firmly believe, for very and for awful emphasis—*thrice*.

The place which Christ in Luke xvi:23, describes is a place where the rich man "lift up his eyes being in torments." That the word *Hades* substituted by the Revisers gives to the Anglo-Saxon a truer and more vivid notion of "torments" than Hell does, what common sense will affirm?

As for the Old Testament, I will contend it, and there are men too in the Holy Church who will help me to contend it—that "Burn unto the lowest hell"—"sorrows of hell"—"pains of hell"—"deeper than hell," mean something more than is brought home to Anglo-Saxon ears by untranslated "Sheol," and something more, and more unutterable than language can depict—than thought can comprehend.

I will contend, that "Sheol" in every one of the thirty-one instances of the Old Testament where, in the authorized version it is now translated "Hell," means, in fact or in figure, all that Anglo-Saxon ever meant by *Hell;* and that men who change that word and blot away that thought, have God to deal with and no judgment of fallible and feeble man. Hell to disappear from the pages of the Old Testament? Why it is the Old Testament whose "Tophet" and whose "everlasting burnings" (Isa 33:14) whose "undying worm and quenchless fire" (Isa lxvi:24) afford the very background and intensest picture of the frightfulness, eternity and instantaneousness after death of Hell Fire. It is the New Testament that preaches "the acceptable year of the Lord," but it is the Old Testament which adds to this, "the *Day of Vengeance* of our God." Hell to disappear from the Old Testament! You never can sustain the doctrine from the New without the undergirding of the Old. Blotted from one Testament, the ground, the reason and the motive of salvation disappear from both.

What then is the grand summing up of this IV. head of the discourse (made p. 16) as to the TENDENCY of the Revision?

1. A general weakening all along the line toward Rome. This must be, if Rome is to furnish the basal document which is to determine our Bible. No wonder then that it has been labored with such untiring earnestness—worthier, far worthier of a better cause—to make out as in the last Presbyterian Review, pp. 334-341, that "the church of Rome is not so corrupt that she has foreefited her right to be called a church." That she must therefore be accepted as a member of the great holy Christian communion, and that her baptism must be regarded as valid. No wonder I say that men have gone up valiantly to Church Courts to overturn if possible, the declaration of the Old School Assembly of 1845 by a vote of 173 to 8, that Rome is apostate and her baptism as a baptism into an apostate system is utterly invalid.*

---

*Assembly's Digest (O. S.) pp. 77, 78, "She neither administers Christian Baptism, nor celebrates the Supper of our Lord.

2. A second Tendency of the Revision is to loosen the Revelation of God from the letter, and to cast it floating out upon the winds. How can God inspire thoughts, ideas, but by words. Did you ever have a thought in your mind, an idea that was not in words? Never. If Inspiration is not verbal, *in the very words* it is nowhere.

3. The tendency is to remove from men that fear of penalty, which, say what we please, is the kingbolt of the Divine Government over the world. Take away the doctrine of Hell-Fire and the world would became one great Sodom. This, this it is above all else that holds the clamp on wicked unbelieving men. A fear of suffering the vengeance of Eternal Fire. The doctrine is "Turn or Burn!" short but unchangeable. If there is no Hell-fire to be saved from, there is no Salvation.

4. The tendency of the Revision will be to rebound. Perhaps the thing has gone far enough and men are beginning to tire of tinkering their Bibles, their Creeds, their sound and tried and wholesome and Scriptural standards. Perhaps the craze for "Criticism" has had its day and the better age of faith—subjection to the mind and will of God is coming in. "Faith," said Luther, "is a sixth sense—above all other senses." The highest exercise of reason is to believe the highest kind of testimony. "There will be no new God, nor new devil," says Spurgeon, "nor shall we ever have a new saviour, nor a new atonement. Why then should we be attracted by the error and nonsense which everywhere plead for a hearing because they are new? To suppose that Theology can be new is to imagine that the Lord Himself is of yesterday. A doctrine lately become true must of necessity be false. Falsehood has no beard, but truth is hoary with an age immeasurable. The old Gospel is the only Gospel. Pity is our only feeling toward those young preachers who cry: 'See my new Theology!' in just the same spirit as little Mary says: 'See my pretty new frock!'"

The time has not come for a New Translation of the Holy Scriptures. The Church is not spiritual enough. The Principle has not been settled, and the Data are not all in.

Now let me say in conclusion—nothing but the fear of God—the hand of God upon me could ever drive me to preach the doctrine of endless Hell-fire.

THE DOCTRINES OF GRACE

I do not love the notion of Hell any more than any other man does. Sensitive as most men to pain, to sorrow and tears, tender of life as any man, and increasingly so of the life of even a worm, I could well resign myself to say "Hades"—to preach, "My friend if you do not repent, if you die without Christ, if you reject this Gospel at my lips, you will return—you will go away into Sheol! You will wander in the shadows of a heathen Hades!" But I cannot preach so and, by God's help I never will.* The wicked shall be turned into *Hell* and all the nations that forget God.

---

*The words "Sheol," (Hebrew) "Hades," (Greek) mean simply *"the invisible world,"* in which are two places and *two places only*—Heaven and Hell. Christ on the Cross, according to the Reformers, sunk under the sorrows of Hell. There, on Him, the Infinite, was poured the penalty infinite. There "the pains of Hell gat hold upon Him." There, "on the tree of the cross, He humbled Himself unto the deepest reproach and *pains of Hell,* both in body and soul, when He cried out with a loud voice *My God, my God! why hast Thou forsaken me!"* The soul of His sufferings were His soul-sufferings. "On the cross," says Calvin, "He endured all hellish agonies in His soul." There, "all God's waves and His billows went over Him." There and not in any Heathen Hades, Romish Purgatory or post-mortem Probation.

When Christ said "It is Finished!" it was finished. When He said "To-day shalt thou be with me in Paradise," that very day He and the saved thief were in Paradise which St. Paul says (2 Cor. xii:2-4) is the "Third Heaven."

RELATIVE VALUE OF THE OLD TESTAMENT

Hosea viii:12

"I have written to him the great things of My law, but they were counted as a strange thing."

The point at issue in the whole controversy with "modern criticism" is, whether the Bible can be placed upon the same plane with other, merely human, literature and treated accordingly, or whether, as a Divine Revelation, it addresses us with a command and sanction? The power of the Book is shaken from the moment we deny its *a priori* binding claim on our belief and obedience. The Book is a royal document, or series of documents issued by the King of kings, and binding upon every subject. The Book, then, is to be received with reverence by one who falls upon his bended knees beneath the only shaft of light which, from unknown eternity, brings to the soul the certainties of God—of His dealings in grace with men, and of a judgment.

The Old Testament is—in some sense—more awful than the New—as it begins with a creation out of nothing—as it thunders from Sinai, and as it prefigures and predicts the momentous facts of Calvary and the Apocalypse.

God the Invisible appears in Genesis and discloses Himself—from the first—in the mystery of three Persons. God's holiness and the certainty that sin shall be punished, is revealed in the awful catastrophes of the Fall, of the Deluge and of Sodom. His mercy is conspicuous in Sacrifice, from Abel's altar down through hectatombs of Blood, to the last sublime tragedy of Golgotha. The wonder and the glory of His purpose shine in the raptures of Enoch and Elijah—in the flaming wheels of Ezekiel, and in those visions of Daniel which picture the confirming of the kingdom in the hands of the triumphant Messiah by the ineffable Ancient of Days.

But it has been represented that the Bible has twisted itself up like a worm from the dust by an Evolution in which the human element is most conspicuous. In place of the doctrine "*I have written to him the great things of My law*" —"*all Scripture, the writing, is given by inspiration of God,*"—in place of the dictum of Christ, "*It is written,*" there has been conceived a notion which lifts inspiration from the writings to the *writers*, and then begins to prate, with owl-like wisdom, of degrees of inspiration—shading these degrees away until—, to use one of the favorite illustrations of this rationalistic school, the feathers at the tips of the wings of the eagle are dead things as compared with the heart of the bird. Certain statements—like the nails on the ends of the fingers, may be excluded as worthless.

Now for the Old Testament,—

If we lose it, we lose our Bibles—if we shake it, we shake our Bibles, for nothing can be more true than that axiom of St. Augustine—*In Vetere Testamento, Novum latet; in Novo Testamento, Vetus patet,*—"In the Old Testament the New lies hidden, in the New the Old is made known." Grant that a human element is in the Old Testament, who can determine how far that element extends? No one. Grant that something has been found out about the Bible, within the last fifty years, that makes it less reliable—less inerrant, in plain English, less free from mistakes than it was,—in some ways, a book that is under *suspicion*, and the result is that the mind is unsettled. Belief rests upon a less secure basis than it did. Grant that some geographical or chronological statements are inaccurate—go a little further, and assume that the men whose names are attached to the books did not write them—that Moses is a fictitious character invented after the captivity—that Deuteronomy was written by reformed Jews who got their ethics in Babylon— that there were no "ethics," i. e. *morality* in the days of the Judges—that the stories of Jephthah and of Jael are atrocious—that the XI of Hebrews might as well be sponged out if one is going back to the Old Testament for examples of any living faith implying spiritual and consistent conduct—that—passing over Isaiah who is a composite character made up of several different men, and Ezekiel and Daniel who are of inferior consideration, the great and perhaps the only authentic prophets are Hosea, Amos and Jeremiah who lived at the close of the Theocracy when

Israel, as a nation, was practically done with and "the times of the Gentiles" were about to come in.

Grant that Ecclesiastes was not written by Solomon but put in the mouth of Solomon as Browning puts reflections into the mouth of Fra Filippo Lippi; and that Job, as a character is perhaps historically as true as Hamlet upon whom Shakespeare's tragedy was founded,— Grant this, and then grant that the story of the Fall itself, on which St. Paul grounds all his theology, is but a myth—or as Westcott and Bishop Temple—not to speak of pronounced heresiarchs—put it, an *allegory* covering a long succession of evolutions which had done their work, in forming man such as he is, before the narrative begins— Grant these things and what becomes of the awful impress of responsibility laid on the conscience by the Sacred Volume? What becomes of the tremendous parallel between the First and Second Adam on which is built the covenant of Grace?

As a counterpoise to a tendency so dangerous and to errors so radical, let us inquire.

I. What is meant by the Old Testament?
II. What is meant by its being inspired?
III. What is its value relative to the New?

I. *What is the Old Testament?*

It is the word of God—the *very* word of *very* God—"I have written to him the great things of my law."

1. The Bible *claims* to be the word of God. No literature in the world can for one instant be compared with it. It is evidently on a plane above the natural.

Nor can anything be alleged against a *supernatural* communication from God. Neither science, nor history, nor criticism, nor any fact we know, nor any postulate we can conjecture, can bear evidence against the Divine origin of the Hebrew Scriptures. There is no reason, and there can be none, why God, who has made man in His own image and capable of communion with Himself should not speak to man and, having taught him letters, *write* to man, in other words, to put His communication in permanent form. The man who denies the supernatural is one who contradicts his own limitations. Either HE is the universe, or there is something outside of him. Either he is his own god or there is a God above him. The inspiration of the Old Testament, including that of the whole Bible, is a matter, first of all, of pure Divine testimony, which leaves us nothing but to receive it. God says, "I am speaking." That ends it. The instant order of the Book to every reader is "Believe or die!"

2. The Book brings with it its authentication. Who would think of standing up under the broad blaze of the noonday sun to deny the existence of the sun? His shining is his authentication.

In like manner the Old Testament, by the supernatural truths which it reveals, by the supernatural facts which it records, by its supernatural appeal to heart and conscience, by the witness of the Holy Ghost, and by its influence in uplifting lands and ages, radiates itself through all horizons as Divine.

3. The Old Testament contains the oldest records of the world—records dating back of all history, of all relics, of all memory or reach of man—records which, in their earliest pages, cannot be confirmed, because there are no data beside them—which run back of the dimmest tradition and which only in later periods begin to receive confirmation, as they universally do, from fragments of Assyrian cylinders and ruins of Egyptian monuments. God, back of all profane history, tells us of the origin of nations, of the Flood, of the antediluvian era, of creation, things otherwise and utterly beyond our ken.

4. The canon or volume of the Old Testament, as we have it, containing thirty-nine books, is identically the text that Christ had, and that He endorses, quoting from its every part.

In the first place, there are no other books in the world, written in Hebrew, which date from before Christ's day.

Again: The volume from which Christ quotes was in existence and identically the same as now, when the Septuagint translation into the Greek was made, 280 years before Christ.

Again: The Hebrew Bible which we have, containing the thirty-nine Old Testament books, has come down to us preserved with a care beyond that ever given to another book.

The Jews cherished the highest awe and veneration for

their sacred writings which they regarded as the "Oracles of God." They maintained that God had more care of the letters and syllables of the Law than of the stars of heaven, and that upon each tittle of it mountains of doctrine hung. For this reason every individual letter was numbered by them and account kept of how often it occurred. In the transcription of an authorized synagogue MS., rules were enforced of the minutest character. The copyist must write with a particular ink, on a particular parchment. He must write in so many columns, of such a size, and containing just so many lines and words. No word to be written without previously looking at the original. The copy, when completed, must be examined and compared within thirty days; if four errors were found on one parchment, the examination went no farther—the whole was rejected. When worn out, the rolls were officially and solemnly burned lest the Scripture might fall into profane hands or into fragments.

The Old Testament, precisely as we have it, was endorsed by Jesus Christ, the Son of God. When he appeared on the earth, 1,500 years after Moses, the first of the prophets, and 400 years after Malachi, the last of them, He bore open testimony to the Sacred Canon as held by the Jews of His time. Nor did he—among all the evils which he charged upon His countrymen—ever intimate that they had, in any degree, corrupted the canon, either by addition, diminution or alteration of any kind.

By referring to the "Scriptures," which He declared "cannot be broken," the Lord Jesus Christ has given His full attestation to all and every one of the Books of the Old Testament as the unadulterated Word of God. In his conversation with the two going to Emmaus, when, beginning at Moses and all the Prophets, He expounded to them in all the Scriptures the things concerning Himself, He gave express endorsement to the whole canon, and to the canon as a whole. Again when—just before His ascension, He said to his apostles, adopting the three-fold division of the Old Testament known to them—"These are the words which I spake unto you while I was yet present with you, that all things must be fulfilled which were written in the *Law of Moses,* and in the *Prophets* and in the *Psalms* concerning Me," He endorsed the Books, one and all. Our Blessed Lord puts "what is written" equal to His own declaration. He saw the Old Testament inspired from one end to the other, divine from one end to the other. Ah! how He valued the sacred text.

Our modern critics, with arrogance which rises to daring impiety, deny to Christ the insight which they claim for themselves. The point right here is this, Did Jesus fundamentally misconceive the character of the Old Testament? Did he take for a created and immediate revelation what was of a slow and ordinary growth? Or was He *dishonest,* and did He make about Abraham, for example, statements and representations which belong only to a geographical myth—a personality which never existed?

The authority of Jesus Christ, God speaking—not from heaven only, but with human lips—has given a sanction to every book and sentence in the Jewish canon, and blasphemy is written on the forehead of any theory which alleges imperfection, error, contradiction or sin in any book in the sacred collection.

The Old Testament was Our Lord's only study book. On it His spiritual life was nurtured. In all His life it was His only reference. Through His Apostles He reaffirmed it. Five hundred and four times is the Old Testament quoted in the New.

5. The whole Jewish nation, down to this day, acknowledge, *without one dissenting voice,* the genuineness of the Old Testament. The Book reflects upon them and condemns them; it also goes to build up Christianity, a system which they hate, and yet, impressed with an unalterable conviction of their divine origin, they have, at the expense of everything dear to man, clung to the Old Testament Scriptures.

6. All churches, everywhere and always, and with one accord, declare the Bible in both Testaments to be the foundation of their creed. All the fathers, Melito, Origen, Cyril, Athanasius, in their lists include the whole thirty-nine books. The Council of Laodicea, held in the year 363, names and confirms them.

7. The books hang together and form one perfect unity which cannot be impaired in the smallest particular without mutilation and loss. The attempt to remove any book or part of a book would at once open an unthought of gap which nothing *but* that book or fragment could fill. A while ago an effort was made to discredit Jonah as fable, but it was found that the Deity of Christ went down with Jonah, that the linchpin between the Testaments fell out with Jonah, and the mass of evidence in favor of the book became so overwhelming that its doughty opponents beat a hasty and cowardly retreat into apology, retraction and silence.

II. *The Old Testament is inspired from end to end*—that is our second point. What do we mean by this?

We mean infallibility and perfection. We mean that the books are of absolute authority, demanding an unlimited submission. We mean that Genesis is as literally the Word of God as are the Gospels—Joshua as is the Acts—Proverbs as are the Epistles—the Song of Solomon as is the Revelation. We mean that the WRITINGS were inspired. Nothing is said in the Bible about the inspiration of the *writers*. It is of small importance to us who wrote Ruth. It is of every importance that Ruth was written by God.

How did God write? On Sinai, He wrote, we are told, with his finger. We are told this in seven different places. "The tables were the work of God," says Moses, "and the writing was the writing of God." "The Lord delivered unto me two Tables of Stone written with the finger of God." Let me think, every time I read the ten commandments, "God's finger traced the square Hebrew characters that make these words. But, if this be true of Exod. XX, then it is true of the whole Canon. The human element vanishes and lays bare the Divine. It is God who writes the Book—a letter and a message straight from heaven. "I have written to him the great things of My Law." On the original parchment every sentence, word, line, mark, point, pen-stroke, jot, tittle, was put there by God.

But God wrote, not only as on Sinai, but also through men. How did He do this?

He did not do it contrary to them: as one would take the

fingers of a wilful schoolboy and force them to make certain marks on a slate or in a copy-book.

God wrote above them, for they themselves "inquired what things they were which the Spirit of Christ which was in them did signify." "Unto whom it was revealed that not unto themselves but unto us did they minister the things which are reported."

God used men with different degrees of style. He made Amos write like a herdsman and David like a poet. He made the difference, provided for it and employed it because He would have variety and adapt Himself to all classes and ages.

He wrote *through* the men. How did He do this? I do not know. The fact, I know, for I am told it. The secret is His own. I read that "holy men of old spake as they were moved"—then they did not choose their own language. I do not know how the electric fluid writes letters on a strip of paper. I do not know how my soul dictates to and controls my body so that the moving of my finger tips is the action of my soul. I do not know how, in regeneration, God does all and I do all. He produces all and I act all, for what He produces is my act.

Inspiration is a matter of Divine testimony. It was God Himself, we are told, who "at sundry times and in divers manners, *spake,* in time past unto the fathers *by* the prophets."

"But there are *variations* in the readings!"

There may be in some cases in the copies—but none in the original—which God made and which He will preserve in spite of all variations. "Forever, O LORD, Thy word is settled in heaven." If settled *there,* earth cannot move it.

"But there are discrepancies—contradictions."

No! Scores of times I have corrected myself, but never God's word. Patience and a larger knowledge will solve every knot. Dr. Hodge of Princeton, says: "Not one single instance of a discrepancy in Scripture has ever been proved."

The Scripture of the Old Testament must be directly inspired because it reveals, behind the act, the inner, secret thoughts and motives. Who but the Searcher of hearts,— what man or angel were competent for this?

The Scripture of the Old Testament, as a revelation, must be free from error, or, if not, it is inferior to certain works of man. Euclid, for instance. Algebra, for instance. He who charges error charges it on God.

The Scripture of the Old Testament must be directly inspired because it reverses human thought and gives God's order—a spiritual order, not man's. Would all the united wisdom of men have led them to relate the history of the creation of the universe in a single chapter, and that of the erection of the Tabernacle in thirteen? The description of the great edifice of the world, would it not seem to require more words than that of a small tent? That would be man's thought. What is God's? The Tabernacle was a figure of the Church, and God would show that the world is less than the Church and was created only as a platform for the Church by which His manifold wisdom is to be made known to principalities and powers.

So far from the Bible being imperfect in its beginnings and growing to be perfect—rising as it advances, from a merely ethnic level to a higher level is, from the first, supernatural and therfore perfect—perfect as God, of whom it is the absolute and inerrant disclosure and transcript. Unchangeable as God is, its *ipse dixit* is final.

The historical books of the Old Testament, as we have them in their order down to II. Kings, are logically and chronologically successive—in the line of God's purpose and His working, as they ought to be—and they form a succinct and continuous history which is supplemented, but not deranged by other books.

The contention of the Modern School is that the books and even their contents are not chronological but simply a congeries of material thrown together by compilers. But never does the name of a compiler appear. No one yet has had imagination enough to invent a plausible name.

According to this theory Moses could not have written Genesis 1 and 2, because the abstract name of God is given in the account of creation but the covenant name *"Jehovah"* when it comes to fellowship with man.

It is said, too, that Abraham was a myth intended to represent a period and tide of emigration. It is said that the story of Joseph was written by two men, one of whom was friendly to Reuben and the other to Judah. It is said that the religious laws and ordinances of the Old Covenant were not given once for all, in permanent form, from Sinai and in the Pentateuch, but grew up under human teachers and by a process of natural development or evolution, so that Deuteronomy is the last of all the books—except perhaps the Psalms, only two of which, the 7th and the 18th, were written by David—the rest were *exilic* and dated from Babylon.

The result of all this is what! To discredit the statement repeated in almost every chapter of Exodus and Leviticus—"And the Lord said to Moses." "As the Lord commanded Moses." To charge Christ with falsehood, who says "Moses said," "Moses taught you," "David says"—quoting as He does not from the 7th and the 18th only, but from the 41st, the 110th, the 118th and other Psalms. The result is to disintegrate the Bible and throw it into heaps of confusion mingled with rubbish—to shake faith to the very foundations and scatter Revelation to the winds. It is to elevate Robertson Smith, Wellhausen, Baur, Astruc, Cheyne and other heretics, who seem to have taken God into their own hands, to a level with the Saviour of men and His prophets, whom they criticise freely. This is not exegesis, it is conspiracy. It is not contribution to religious knowledge, it is *crime!*

Think of the amazing, the stupendous difference between Christ quoting from a human compilation, or from the living Oracles of God! "I came not to destroy," He says, "but to fulfil"—to fulfil what? A hap-hazard collection of Ezra's time—made up of fragmentary documents of men, some of whom had an inspiration little above that of Browning and Tennyson!

III. What then, is *the relative value of the Old Testament?*

1. It is of equal value with the New. We have seen that every word of it was penned by God. The words of God are of an equal value.

2. The Old Testament impresses the most awful truths concerning the personality and holiness of God and the certainty of His law and its penalty.

In the Old Testament God is seen above, apart from the universe—not immanent, but pre-manent—Self Existent, while the universe depends upon Him, creating it, controlling it and working in and through it.

In the Old Testament the holiness of God is seen reflected in His law and its penalty. Sinners against nature die. The Antediluvians die. The Sodomites die. Nadab and Abihu die. Leprosy seizes Gehazi. On Sinai the Law thunders as nowhere else in the whole Bible. The mountain rocks under the presence and voice of Jehovah. Hell in its most awful disclosure lies open in the Old Testament. The steps of men are seen "taking hold on hell." "The wicked shall be turned into hell." "The sinners in Zion are afraid; fearfulness hath surprised the hypocrites: who among us shall dwell with the devouring fire? Who among us shall dwell with Everlasting burnings?"

3. The Old Testament teaches and impresses each one of the doctrines of grace.

The doctrine of *depravity*. It shows sin a serpent in the Garden. It declares that every imagination of the thought of man's heart is only evil continually. "Behold I was shapen in iniquity," says David, "and in sin did my mother conceive me." St. Paul, to emphasize the depravity of man, quotes everywhere from the Old Testament.

The doctrine of *election* is taught everywhere in the Old Testament. "Jacob have I loved, Esau have I hated." "Blessed is the man whom Thou chooest and causest to approach unto Thee." Israel is everywhere a chosen people.

The doctrine of *justification* by *faith* is explicitly taught in the Old Testament. "Even as David also describeth the blessedness of the man unto whom God imputeth righteousness without works, saying: Blessed is the man whose iniquities are forgiven and whose sins are covered."

The doctrine of *regeneration*—of a new heart, of a new birth, of a new spirit—is taught in the Old Testament. "Create within me a clean heart, O God, and renew a right spirit within me." "A new heart also will I give unto you and a new spirit will I put within you." Christ tells Nicodemus, a master in Israel, that he ought to have known this.

The doctrine of the *preservation of the Saints* is everywhere taught in the Old Testament. "The mountains shall

THE DOCTRINES OF GRACE 99

depart and the hills be removed before God will ever break His promise to save His people who trust Him." "Israel shall be saved in the Lord with an everlasting salvation."

Had we the Old Testament alone it would be sufficient to save us. I myself was converted on that very part of Isaiah which the critics say he did not write. Men have been converted by the millions and are now in heaven who never knew anything but the Old Testament. They found God in it, and so may you and I.

4. The Old Testament throws a light upon Christ and upon the whole Christian system without which the New Testament could not be understood. Atonement looms in Abel's altar and runs on to the Great Substitute to be stricken for His people, upon whom the Lord hath laid the iniquity of us all. "The life of the flesh is in the Blood." says Leviticus, "and I have given it to you upon the altar to make an atonement for the soul—for it is the Blood that maketh an atonement for the soul." Blood drips from each page of the Old Testament. Each letter stars crimson. What is all this, if not Christ? The Old Testament is the dictionary and key to the New. If *with* the Old Testament and without Christ we were helpless, equally—*without* the Old Testament and with Christ—we should be helpless. I beseech you, therefore, Brethren, beware of what is called "the modern school."

5. The entire Old Testament is *typical*. "*All* these things," says St. Paul, were types—τυποι, ταυτα δε παντα. There is a mystical sense in the Scripture which ought to make men afraid of it. God and His purpose runs through it all. Melchizedeck, Joshua, David, Solomon, Jonah, all typify Christ. Christ was the Manna in the wilderness. Christ was the Stricken Rock. Hagar is the Covenant of works, Sarah is the Covenant of grace. Turn the pages reverently, prayerfully, I beg you, for these and ten thousand other mysteries, undiscovered yet, lie hidden in these Oracles of God. There is a closeness and a detail of correspondence between the story of ancient Israel and the experience of the Christian soul and the life of the Christian Church which is the result of no accident—the caprice of no compiler.

> "Sweet fields beyond the swelling flood,
> Stand dressed in living green,"

is no pictured fancy of what the Old Testament reveals.

6. The whole Old Testament is *prophetic* of Christ. "These are they which *testify* of Me." Each phase of His suffering is depicted down to the casting of lots for His vesture: each phase of His glory from His triumphant entry into Jerusalem upon an ass's colt to the consummation of His Messianic and Davidic throne. St. Paul tells us that the Gospel of God to which he was separated, had been "promised before by the prophets in the Holy Scripture concerning His Son Jesus Christ our Lord." St. John tells us that "the testimony of Jesus is the *spirit* of prophecy." The whole Old Testament, from Genesis to Malachi, spells "Jesus," "Jesus only."

> "Christ is the end, as Christ was the beginning;
> Christ the beginning, for the end is Christ."

7. The entire scheme of right and sound theology depends upon the Old Testament. St. Paul argues in Romans and in Galatians that Abraham was not justified by works but by simple *faith* and therefore that we may be. He argues in Romans 5 that if the whole race fell by representation in Adam as their federal head—if we were condemned on the ground of what ONE man did, without having a hand in it—then there is a loophole by which we can be saved on the ground of what another Man—a second Adam—has done, without having a hand in that either.

May God enable us to seize upon that loophole of escape and rescue and to shun the errors which are in the air all around us and are drifting so much of the misdirected zeal and learning of the present generation into a blind alley, from which there is no safe issue but return.

COSMOGONY: A STUDY OF THE FIRST TWO CHAPTERS OF GENESIS

"In the beginning, God created the Heavens and the Earth!" Here are the Pillars of Hercules through which we pass from Time with all its changes, into Eternity—a shoreless, changeless sea. Here are the frontiers of human exploration, beyond which rolls and surges the illimitable Ocean of Deity, self-existent, blessed forever and independent of all creatures.

The first utterance of the Bible fixes it that matter is not eternal. That there was a point when the universe was not and when God, by simple fiat, brought it into being. So that, as the apostle says, He called the Existent out of the non-existent—the visible from that which had no visibility. In other words, God made the world out of nothing—an awful nothing—the idea of which we cannot comprehend. A lonely and a solitary Worker, out of emptiness, He created fullness—out of what was not, all things—getting from Himself the substance as well as the shaping—the fact as well as the how.

In the beginning, God created the Heavens and the Earth! He had to tell us that, for He *only* was there. He had to *tell* us that, but—being told, we, at once, believe it, for everything outside the self existent must have a beginning. Matter must have had a beginning, for—push its molecules back as far as you will, either matter was the egg out of which God was hatched or God hatched matter. Can there be any question as to which of these is true?

"In the beginning, God created the Heavens and the Earth." If this first sentence is unauthentic, the whole Bible is untrue and for six thousand years men have been duped and deluded who have loved and cherished its teachings.

If this first sentence is, however, to be relied on, then God is the author and the book is true in all its chain of history and doctrine—true throughout.

The credibility of the Bible, then, depends upon the truth of the First Chapter of Genesis. If that chapter is clean and clear in all its statements, so is the Book. If that chapter contains "a few small scientific lies," then the Book is a caries of deceptions from cover to cover. Thus we are either Christians or sceptics!

The Bible says: "In the beginning God created the heavens and the earth." Heathen philosophy has always said: In the beginning the universe commenced to *evolve* itself. The Bible says: "God created man male and female and, from one pair, *one race.*" Ancient philosophy knew nothing about this. Each tribe, each nation had its own local traditions, deities and legends. The original bond uniting all people, in one blood, was unknown. Each nation was supposed to have sprung directly from the earth, or to have emigrated from a region where their ancestors so sprung. Outside of the Bible nowhere was there a notion of the human race as a unit, nor of its having any other than an *autochthonous*,—*i. e.*, a material and earthly origin.

It has been claimed that no essential injury is done to Christian faith by concessions made to modern criticism—that if one believes in redemption, it is of small account what he believes of creation. But men who speak so rashly, overlook the fact that creation is the basis of redemption,—that there must be man and man FALLEN before there can be man *saved*—and that the belief in creation depends entirely upon the acknowledgment of Genesis, as a historical document. The First Book of the Scripture is the germ of the whole—the root out of which grows every idea that is found in the Bible. It is not possible to kill the germ—to hurt the root without destroying the tree.

The Book of Genesis then, occupies a position of preeminent value and sacredness. With what an awe should we unfold its pages. But for this Book, man would not know how he had been formed, nor for what purpose—he would not know that he was in the image of God created with the promise and the prospect of an everlasting life. The earlier chapters of Genesis, by revealing to man what manner of being he is, and what are his relations to God, lay the foundations of all true piety—all saving knowledge and all real and genuine religion.

THE DOCTRINES OF GRACE

"In the beginning, God created." This destroys the eternity of matter, *but*—matter once created, there is a choice in describing its progress.

One thing: as to what is left out. A chasm of ages on ages splits between the first verse and the second. "In the beginning, God created the heavens and the earth, *But* the earth was *Tohu vah Vohu,* without form and void.

It was not created so, for God creates nothing imperfect, and the prophet Isaiah expressly says, "He created it not *Tohu*"—it was not created without form and void. Then there had been a change and a lapse in it.

Here, then, between the first and second verses, comes in the history and fall of angels. That must be passed by for the present. Undoubtedly God could have stopped to describe the heavens—angels and archangels, cherubim and seraphim, thrones and principalities and powers—the manner and the reason of Satan's fall and how he drew legions after him into the abyss, plunging our solar system, his special province, into chaos.

But to have stopped on this would have been to confuse everything. We do not put syntax into an A. B. C. book —nor the Binomial Theorem into the first pages of algebra. To have delayed on this would have involved the use of heavenly language which we could not understand, or if earthly words were used, our thoughts must have been wholly diverted from ourselves, our frailty, our guilt and need, to an unwholesome speculation about things which do not concern us.

Because the Bible is addressed to the inhabitants of earth, it comes down to earth as soon as possible, and speaks to us in a terrestrial language. If, then, it gives us the facts about the earth, as they occurred,—and if it states them according to *appearances* without going behind the appearances—if it speaks of the sun's rising and setting, that is only common-sense, it is only speaking as the wisest astronomers among us do, who know perfectly well that the sun does not rise nor set at all, but that the Earth turns toward and away from him—and yet they talk of sunrise and of sunset, too.

The Bible, to be useful to us, must speak according to appearances. If one were describing a panorama, he would not confuse his description by going back of the moving picture to the machinery which was working behind it, nor proceed to tell how the artist came to conceive the thought of a panorama, nor when nor how he planned the part and details of the moving scene. A person coming home to you and attempting to give you some distinct notion of the panorama itself would not philosophize but would start with the painting, as it starts and follow it, in memory and in narrative, as it unrolls before his eyes.

Such is God's method in describing the Creation—His simple, sublime and common-sense method—a method involving the soundest philosophy—if we wish to employ such a word.

For suppose that, instead of giving us a popular and easy book, God had set forth to give us an abstract and scientific one,—from what point of observation shall He speak? Shall He start from the sun and tell us that the earth is a globe, and give us its relations to the sun? Or shall He go back of and above the sun and speak from Alcyone and tell us all about other solar systems and their circulations in the heavens? Shall He speak in such a way as to be intelligible to the age of Shem, or of Ptolemy, or of Copernicus or to that of some later and future astronomer who shall have discovered more than they knew?

Besides: where, in all this, were a revelation concerning God Himself, and our relations to Him and especially as fallen creatures who need to be saved?

As De Quincy has suggested, it would have been impossible for any messenger from God to have descended to the communication of mere worldly scientific truth.

First. Because such a descent would have degraded and neutralized his mission by pandering to profitless and dissipating curiosity.

Again: it would have raised disputes in which all spiritual truth would have been lost. Suppose the speaker to have made the statement that the earth is moving at the rate of one thousand miles an hour,—one man cries out, "Ridiculous—I do not feel it move." A discussion begins which puts a pause to anything further. The inspired speaker or writer is ruined with his audience by stating a scientific truth in advance of them. He feeds them with meat and not with milk which they are able to bear.

Then, again: The Bible must not teach anything which man can teach himself. A Revelation from God is given to tell us—not what we do not yet know, but what we cannot, without it, by any possibility, find out.

What we can find out by study, investigation and discovery, God leaves us to find out. That is His wise arrangement for enlarging and developing our powers. Nor will He interfere with that arrangement. He will not come into the world to tell us about astronomy, steam, electricity and chemical elements. We must, for ourselves, invent the telescope—the condensing cylinder—the battery, the retort. God will not dishonor Himself by descending into the arena of science to make Himself man's rival and to contend with him—so to say—"for His own prizes." A Revelation has not come into the world for the purpose of showing to indolent men what, by faculties already given, they may show to themselves, but, to shine in upon their moral darkness and disclose things wholly supernatural and beyond the ken or reach of human powers,—facts, like the Trinity—Incarnation—Salvation, and Eternal Justice burning to the depthlessness of hell.

So, then, to do us any good, the Bible must speak to men on earth in a terrestrial language and, beginning with the plain statement of necessary facts, go straight forward, leading man—with light enough from the very first to save him, on into the vast disclosures of the Scheme of Grace, as he is able to bear them.

This is the Common-Sense of the First Chapter of Genesis—The fact of an instantaneous and perfect creation is stated.

Then—omitting the fall of angels, with the catastrophe which it involved to our earth, and the satanic forms of Saurians and other horrible reptiles into which the fallen angels were cast,—the second verse in contrast takes up the earth in collapse and in six days builds it up again. The Hebrew verb, *bara*, "to create from nothing," is used in the first verse, but in all the succeeding verses, with two remarkable exceptions—the creation of animal life on the fifth day, and the creation of the human soul on the sixth— another verb, which signifies "to modify" or "shape," is constantly employed. God creates only at crises and from necessity. Then He revamps and moulds to higher forms, and varied uses. So we read, in the first verse, *bara,* "He created," but, afterward, *asah,* "He made or stretched out the firmament," and so on.

As to the days of Genesis I., there is no geology in them —that is to say, there are no ages upon ages of Silurian and other changes. Whatever geological phenomena we may not refer to the flood, and it will no doubt largely account for them,—whatever other cataclysms and melting of the rocks, and whatever reptilian age there may have been, occurs between the first and second verses of the chapter. There, in the split chasm and in the silence, which God Himself has left unfilled, Geology has all the room it wants in which to work.

As to the *length* of the Creation days. Men have stoutly contended that they were not days—that the Hebrew *yom* does not mean days, but indefinite periods.

In reply, it is easy for the Christian scholar to say: The word *yom* might possibly mean an indefinite period, if there were any necessity or call for this—since "one day is, with the Lord, as a thousand years, and a thousand years as one day." But there is no necessity, but great confusion, in making the Genesis days each of them one thousand years long:

1. In the first place there is the "evening" and the "morning"—the sunset of the first day and the sunrise of the next described. Diurnal days are twenty-four hours, not one thousand years long.

2. No solid reason whatever appears why the word "day" should be taken or explained in a figurative, metaphorical sense. If God meant "indefinite periods," there is a Hebrew word for it. If He meant years He could easily have said "years," or "centuries," or "millenniums," or "eons." If He said "days," He means days—He means us to get that impression.

3. The work of reconstruction could have been instantaneous—light, darkness, sea, land, plants, animals and man might have been brought into being at once, had God willed it. Why not, then, in successive stages, marked by

revolutions of the globe? It is not said, in Genesis I., that the present arrangement of our world, as a suitable place for man, was a work of creation or making out of nothing. It is distinctly said that "in the beginning, God created the heavens and the earth," and that afterward, in six days He made material and created things to *assume* their present form. A man may make a table or a sofa in six days, but no one supposes he made the wood in six days. On the first day the earth was without form, but the materials for rearrangement were there. On entering a foundry, we often see a large number of broken pieces of machinery ready to be recast into different shapes and machines from what they were before. So with the earth in chaos on the first day. All the forms of the preceding plan had been broken up, awaiting the word which was to call them afresh into shape and beauty. The materials for the re-arrangement were there—then in six days the re-arrangement was completed.

In six literal, natural days, for:

4. If the *Sun*, which had been obscured before by darkness and mephitic vapors, appeared again the fourth day, then the first three days were common, ordinary days, and then, too, the fifth, the sixth, and the seventh. And,

5. It would have been impossible to guard the keeping of the Fourth Commandment on any other than a twenty-four-hour basis. God commands us to keep the Sabbath because He kept it,—not because He rested for a thousand years after creating Adam, before He did anything else,—leaving Adam and Eve one thousand years in Paradise,—and not because He is indefinitely keeping it now, but because He actually and definitely kept it then and caused Adam and Eve and all the animals and all creation to keep it as the last and fitting *finale*—when He had finished His work.

Now, take it the other way, and read the Fourth Commandment in the critical light: "Remember the seventh indefinite period to keep it holy. Six indefinite periods shalt thou labor and do all thy work, but the seventh indefinite period thou shalt not do any work, thou nor thy son nor thy daughter, . . . for, in six indefinite periods the Lord made heaven and earth, the sea, and all that in them is, and rested the seventh period, wherefore the Lord blessed the seventh indefinite period and hallowed it"—That is to say, there is no such thing as a Sabbath of twenty-four hours and the Commandment placed as the very keystone and decalogue is shown an absurdity! But,

6. The controversy concerning the Sabbath, which commenced with the apostasy and has continued ever since, was foreseen before the creation and it was for that very reason, according to the Scriptures, that the six days of twenty-four hours each, were made the divisions of the Genesis week. "In six days the Lord made heaven and earth, the sea and all that in them is, and rested the seventh day, WHEREFORE, the Lord blessed the Sabbath day and hallowed it." In confirmation of this, we find the Lord saying: "Verily, My Sabbaths ye shall keep for it is a *sign* between Me and you throughout your generations. Six days may work be done, but in the seventh is the Sabbath of rest holy unto the Lord. It is a *sign* between Me and the children of Israel forever. For in six days the Lord made heaven and earth, and on the seventh day He rested." The Sabbath was instituted in Paradise and ever since has been a sign and a testimony that in the six natural days preceding its institution the Lord was working and that He rested on the consecrated seventh day.

7. The Sabbath Law founded on Genesis I. lies in the very constitution of moral being. God has so adjusted man and nature that one-seventh of our time must be given to Him, or the world goes to ruin. Heathenism depends on getting away from this law. Heathenism has no sabbath, and heathenism speaks its own condemnation. True religion depends on getting back to the sabbath. So far from being an appendage to the decalogue, the Fourth Commandment is basal. It is the center and root. If there be no periodic and appointed time of rest, then there can be no proper worship of God—no general agreement as to any time; and no proper opportunity in which, apart from worldly cares, to consider what is due to God and what is due to man. *Idolatry* goes with the abolition of the sabbath, and disobedience, murder and uncleanness go with the abolition of the sabbath. On the Fourth Commandment hangs the whole Law. It is fundamental—so fundamental as to be the ground-work of everything.

God only knows the exact proportion of time which we should offer as a tribute to Him. He requires the one-seventh part of our lives. He has fixed the proportion as He has fixed seven notes in music—seven colors in the spectrum—seven wave-beats in light and in the ocean. The number seven, called by the fathers *aeiparthenos,* "always a Virgin," follows the Lamb whithersoever He goeth. It is the Lord's Day and He made it and we will rejoice in it and be glad.

It is a day—not a century. How could a dying creature work six centuries and then do nothing for a hundred years? It is a day—not a year—how much more suitable for man, frail transitory pilgrim here, to have rest often—than to work incessantly six years and then do nothing!

The First Chapter of Genesis lies at the bottom of everything. It founds creation on God, and religion on the Sabbath. Take away the first—creation, and you have *chaos*. Not perfection, but chaos, and chaos without a fall—unaccountable chaos—call it atoms—call it fire mist—swell out your pomposity and call it the *Nebular Hypothesis*—in English, "the Nebular Guess,"—Call it what you please—it is something without a First Cause. It is rank heathen speculation and darkness. Take away the second—the sabbath, and there is no meeting-ground on which to worship, and the knowledge of God, even if a God be granted, is lost.

The second Chapter of Genesis makes a transition. It passes not only from the material creation to the moral creation, but from God, as abstract, to God in touch with man and in covenant.

This involves,
1. A change in the Divine Name.
2. The Nobility of Man as created. And,

1. *A change in the Divine Name.*

On reading the First Chapter, one will have noticed that the uniform word for the Almighty is "God." But when we come to the Second Chapter of Genesis another title is introduced. It is no longer Elohim, "God," but *Jehovah Elohim,* "Lord-*God.*"

The critics have seized upon this to assert two different

documents, by different writers,—one of which they call the *"Elohistic,"* document, and the other the *"Jehovistic,"*—their aim being to prove that Moses was not the only writer of Genesis.

The difficulty with Higher Criticism is that it disbelieves in advance and the reason of this too frequently is that it is working with a brain whose crooked and vapid conclusions are guided by a heart averse to God—at enmity with God and working every way to get rid of Him. It is remarkable that the only thing which God claims of man is his heart—a humble, docile, teachable spirit. It is by this—*i. e.,* through a right and proper instinct in him, that all just conceptions and explanations of Scripture will be attained.

Now, to a simple, child-like, appreciative faith, this change from *"God"* to *"Lord God"* is most significant and congruous and beautiful. "God," the abstract God of nature—the *material,* is not the God of man—the *moral.* And so, as Moses advances to this moral, he reveals a more intimate and tender side of the Divine character. The word "LORD" is employed—a word which means Owner, Possessor—One who treasures and cherishes, One whose affections are centered upon and wrapt up in what is to be made. Before, it was creation in *power,*—now it is creation in *love* and the word changes from "God" to "Lord"—a gracious, sovereign, Preserver, Protector and Benefactor.

Let me go even further here, and suggest that the word "LORD" may refer to the Second Person of the Holy Trinity. who at this point discloses Himself. God the Father has been seen by no man, but God the Son constantly appears as the Jehovah of the Old Testament—the Angel or the Messenger Who is the Lord—the Word by Whom were created all things.

It is wonderfully glorious to glimpse the shadow of the Lord Jesus thus thrown upon the foreground in the creation of man. How near to us we find Him away back among the trees of the Garden. How spontaneously rise to our lips the words so familiar

> "Jesus, Thy name I love
> All other names above,
> JESUS, MY LORD!"

See then a reason for the change in these words as we pass on to the second chapter. See how consistent Moses is—and why should he not be consistent? Modern Exegetes may contend that several writers have shared in the composition of Genesis, but—apart from the absurdity of a *mosaic* which is not Mosaic, the ordinary Christian will never consent to lose Moses,—the man with an unparalleled public—with an unparalleled vocation and unparalleled endowments—the man endorsed by Christ Himself as its author, from under the foundation, of the book. The Book depends on Moses—on his authority and name. Moses wrote the Pentateuch—the whole Pentateuch and the Pentateuch as a whole. We must either so receive it, or be driven finally to reject it all—from Genesis to Deuteronomy.

2. It is by this admirable introduction, this significant alteration of the Divine Name, that we are led to apprehend the true *nobility of man* as the offspring, the product of a Divine forethought and affection. It was the creation of a being having a Divine element,—it was the creation of a perfect being,—it was the creation of something responsible.

(1) It was the creation of a being having a *Divine element*.

It is not easy to rise to this conception in our thoughts at once, and because the Divine element has been so sadly lost by us in the fall. "The natural man receiveth not the things of the Spirit of God, neither can he know them, because they are spiritually discerned." And it is a sufficient evidence of the fact that we have fallen, that we figure Adam as, at most, a blithesome, innocent child of nature, a sort of handsome or unhandsome savage. Whereas, a sound reflection would teach us that a being able and warranted to hold communion with the Great First Cause of all things, must stand, *ipso facto,* on an elevation vastly higher than that of the greatest men of any succeeding economy—that he must see light in God's light and be himself, a little god reflecting God and surveying life and the world from a vantage ground far loftier than that of our supremest genius.

Man was an *immediate* creation, the recipient of a Divine

nature and of a higher Divine nature even than the angels. So that there is no link between man and the animal such as fond and foolish evolutionists have dreamed. I know that it has been asserted that the monkey is the embryo human —so that if you keep a baboon long enough it will develop itself into a man. But this is to imagine that an ape can lift itself into a Divine nature and become god-like. A fancy not only absurd, but profane. The man who makes himself, in thought, an ape, is guilty of sacrilege. He sins against the Temple of the Holy Ghost. So patent is this that Professor Virchow, the foremost of German scientists, has said: "I have nothing to do with the conception that man emerged from the animal—for, as a matter of fact, not one link of transition has ever been found." Below the lowest limit in man there drops a gulf that is infinite.

Besides: if man was once a beast, he may become bestial again—since nothing is easier than to relapse, to fall backward. An outlook sufficiently appalling, one would suppose, to make even error see that it has overshot itself.

And further: the uniqueness of nobility in man appears in the *position* which he was to occupy here below. God had already made the earth and formed its living tenantry, but there still lacked the Crown and Capital, the ruler and the priest of all. Man must be made for God, since earth was made for man,—for man to control it—to stand with his hand upon the tiller and to steer the floating orb on to its physical and moral destiny. What sort of a being must that be—the *Eye* of creation to see the Invisible who governs it—the *Ear* of creation to hear and to obey His bidding—the High Priest of creation, to gather in his censer and to offer up the incense of its varied and united worship? What wonder that we read that God, so to say, imparted Himself to him—that what He would not stoop to do to an animal, He stoops to do to a man, when, kissing him upon his lips, He breathes into his nostrils the ineffable *nishamah*, making him immortal as God!

That brings us to notice,

(2) The Creation of man was that of a *perfect* being. Not of a being confirmed in holiness, but of a being holy, although unconfirmed. It was the beautiful Vase of the

Potter finished, but with its clay not yet porcelain—its colors not burned in.

Adam had all the perfection he would ever have, or could have—only he must STAY what he was.

As a moral being, he was perfect in that highest of all perfection—*Insight*, Intuition,—the faculty by which the soul, illumined by the light of God, has an immediate perception of character as moral.

We find traces of this wonderful endowment still, especially in women and little children. God has given woman a defense against moral evil in her instinct. She need not be deceived. She must blind herself to be deceived. The instinctive knowledge of character manifested by the youngest child is also a proof of this innate inheritance— that singular attraction to or repulsion from a stranger which a child will show even before it can speak.

Adam had this in the highest degree. No cloud of sin shut out the light of God from his soul, but, full of light, and turning light on everything around him, he could instinctively discern the Mind of God in all His works and appropriately name and describe them all, in agreement with the purpose of God in creating them.

This is the deep spiritual meaning of the nineteenth and twentieth verses, where we are told that "the Lord God brought every beast of the field, and every fowl of the air to Adam to see what he would name them, and whatsoever Adam called every living creature, that was the name thereof,"—so clear was his intuition that he made no mistake.

Adam, then, knew the *serpent* and the fearful danger which lay below that subtlety—that finesse which, while still innocent, is yet so close to falseness, to obliquity, to twist and to deceit, as to become the aptest instrument for Satan.

Adam perfectly knew the *serpent* as he passed him in review among the other animals. And, endowed with this perception of character, Eve would have at once seen into that of her tempter, had her eyes not been occupied with the beauty of the deadly fruit.

Man was made perfect. His body was of dust, but it was the efflorescence of dust, just as the diamond is made of charcoal, but is yet the diamond. His soul was made in the likeness of God—immortal as God is—holy as God is—

happy as God is,—in all respects, in intellect, imagination, feelings, will, conformed to God.

And—of this perfection, his external appearance was an expression not only in the loftiness of his brow and the majesty of his mien, but in the halo of light thrown about him. This is the meaning of the words: "They were naked and were not ashamed. They wore no clothing, but were not therefore without effulgence shining from them and around them which wrapped them in a radiant and translucent cloudy robe—and in a certain lovely way obscured their outlines. It is contrary to nature and it is repulsive to us that anything should be unclothed and absolutely bare. Each bird has its plumage and each animal its coat, and there is no beauty if the covering be removed. Strip the most beautiful bird of its feathers, and, though the form remain unchanged, we no longer admire it.

We conceive, then, that artists are wholly at fault and grossly offend against purity when they paint the human form unclothed and plead as an excuse the case of Adam in Eden. They fail to understand the wondrous meaning of the passage. Could the animals in all their splendid covering coats have bowed down as to the Vicegerents of God,—before beings wholly unclothed? Should Adam, the Crown and the King of Creation, be the only living thing without a screen? Impossible. To the spiritual sense there certainly is a hint of something about our first parents that impressed and overawed the animal creation and was an all-sufficient reason why—so far from being ashamed, they should rather be in danger of an undue exaltation.

What was that thing? What, in the light of other Scriptures, could it have been? What, but that shining forth like the sun which describes the body of the resurrection? If the face of Moses so shone by reflection that the children of Israel were afraid to come nigh him,—how much more must the indwelling Spirit of God in Adam and Eve have flung around them a radiance which made all creation do them reverence as they approached—beholding in them the Image and likeness of the Lord God Almighty—glorious in brightness—shining like a sun!

This explains the expression, "They were not ashamed." It also explains what is said of them after they sinned:

"They ate of the fruit of the forbidden tree," and as they ate, the light within them dimmed and shone out no more. Their halo had vanished, and the Holy Spirit of righteousness which had been to them a covering of transcendent light and purity withdrew and they saw and felt that they were stript and bare and naked, and, shivering in the unclothing, they feared and fled away into the thick woods to hide there.

Man thus created perfect, had perfect *surroundings*. He was in the enjoyment of two things, society and abundance. Adam had an equal and a kindred spirit to be his companion, and to both it was said: "Be fruitful and multiply and replenish the earth and subdue it." Go on from better to better and from success to success. These two things, society and success, are the sum of earthly good.

But,

(3) The creation of man was that of something *responsible*. That is the higher meaning of the Garden and the Tree. For is not man set before us as a being whose perfection consists in exercising self-control and in accepting limits? The fish of the sea—the birds of heaven roamed at their will, through ocean and through air; the beasts grazed where they would, and this unrestrained life of theirs showed that they were far removed from God and from His covenant.

But now: When God creates a sovereign of the world in His own likeness—one who is to be His Vicegerent, one who is to respond to the mind of God by willing as He wills and accepting His limitations—a Garden is fenced in, and man, though lord of the whole earth, is not permitted to roam recklessly at will, but is set to fix the center and the nucleus of outer circles of dominion in a holy and a settled home. He is to begin with a garden and prove that he can dress it and keep it. For if a man know not how to rule his own house, how shall he control the destinies of a Church which is to fill the world? The fruits of the Garden also were to be man's for food, but there must be a limit also to his appetite. Of one tree he was not to eat.

He was thus confronted by law. The fear of the Lord, which is the beginning of wisdom, was implanted in him.

and it was upon his subjection to and dependence upon the Divine will that his future was suspended.

With these sublime Chapters—the opening words of the inspired Volume—before us, let us now draw from them certain corollaries and conclusions—and,

1. How can we know about the origin of things save as we are taught by One who was in existence before them? *As no creature can rise above its experience, so no creature can know creation.* We cannot have the thought or know the fact save as we receive it on testimony which is Divine. That makes it that, from the very first, the Bible, transcending all other books, comes down from above, bringing its own light. It makes it that we must receive the revelation as from God or grope forever in darkness.

2. Creation—a fact, *settles and moulds all our theology.* If we believe that by an evolution of mere nature, there can be the spiritual, we shall have a religion of reforms, of efforts, of self-manufacture, of endeavor to work the "old man" over into the "new." But if we believe that the development of the old man, however strenuous, will be only worse and worse; then we are thrown back on God. If we believe that nature is one thing and grace another and that the natural man cannot receive the things of the Spirit of God; then we shall see how perfectly in accord with the doctrine of an instant creation is the doctrine of an instant regeneration—in which something is given and infused and imparted which was not in the man before. Then we shall see how consistent with God's work from the beginning, is the statement of the apostle. "If any man be in Christ, he is *kaine ktisis* a new creation—old things have passed away; behold all things are become new."

Evolution is the blank denial and destruction of the Christian system. Neither in whole, nor in part, will orthodox men ever admit a development anti-vital. Conception, the beginning of natural life, is a flash—the soul, a direct impartation from God—a creation from nothing. So is the spiritual life—the Divine nature,—it is something formed out of the breath of the Eternal God and breathed into my soul.

3. The Bible teaches that *man is the noblest being in the universe.* That there is no possible computation of what

God meant for him and means for him yet,—first to control himself—then the garden of his own house—then the world—then the universe. Destiny how overwhelming! How in such a prospect does the question press upon me— "What shall it profit a man if he shall prefer his own will— if he shall gain the whole world—as Adam gained the apple in his way, not God's way, and lose his own soul?" And,

4. The Chapters show that *the entire controversy between God and man is one of* WILL *depending upon faith, or unfaith.* There was nothing in the forbidden tree itself— whether it were a fig tree or not—to injure. The point was, would man believe God and obey Him simply because he was told to? He refused. His will clashed with God's and that ended it. He was divided from God and God could use him no more.

Here looms before us,

5. *The Great Principle of Faith.* "By faith we understand that the worlds were made,"—by faith we understand the new birth by the Spirit—by faith we trust in Christ and take Him as the Tree of Life. Our Lord so put it in His interview with Nicodemus. He said, "Ye must be born again—a mystery," and then He pointed to the Serpent on the pole. And St. John continues, "Whosoever believeth that Jesus is Christ, is born of God." Adam lost Paradise by *doubt;* we recover it, in grand reversal, by a *faith* which overcomes the world.

And, if this be so, then the end of philosophy, as of religion, is *to believe.* Then the highest exercise of a creature's reason is to receive the testimony of His Creator, and he who cannot believe gets not one step in God's direction. Then faith takes God's Word as true and does not recognize criticism—the pulling down of Revelation—as any proper department of knowledge. Then faith is *positive* and criticism a halting negation: so far from adding anything, it shows itself a perishing diminuendo—a perpetual subtraction, the attenuating process of which was well described by three cartoons I saw the other day and underneath them these three legends:

First Cartoon and First Higher Critic: "The Bible in its

present mutilated and adulterated state needs a vast amount of work to make it serviceable."

Second Cartoon and Second Higher Critic: "It is a mistake to cast aside so much of ancient lore. All it needs is to be *scientifically* understood."

Third Cartoon and Third Higher Critic: "I have disposed of all the rest of the Bible, but I don't see anything the matter with the *covers*."

JONAH, THE KEYSTONE OF THE TESTAMENTS

Luke xi:29

"And when the people were gathered thick together, He began to say, This is an evil generation, they seek a sign and there shall no sign be given it, but the sign of Jonas the prophet."

Jonah has a peculiar place among the prophets. He was a very early prophet; in fact he may be called the father of prophecy, since he is the oldest, or first of all the prophets who have left writings behind them—his, a book penned by his own hand.

The book is so unique; it is such a blending of the supernatural with the familiar, such an interposition of God in events, such a disclosure of human nature in the prophet—a book so profound in its spiritual mysteries, so progressive in its forecast of broader horizons, that, small as it is in its compass, it is undoubtedly the Keystone of the two Testaments—one wall of the arch of Revelation, the Old Testament, built up on one side to meet it, and the other wall of the arch, the New Testament, built up on the other side to meet it, while, at the point of junction, it drops in, wedgelike, to bind them in unison. Jonah clasps Christ in the Old Testament; Christ clasps Jonah in the New.

It is to this extraordinary and exceptional character of the Book of Jonah that we may attribute the fact that in all ages, the sharpest and most skilful, the bitterest and most artfully concealed opposition of skeptical rationalism has been arrayed against it.

The method of approach has usually been that of ridicule. There is just enough of the bizarre in the stupendous Miracle, around which the Book clusters, to provoke a sneer, and suggest an excuse for stigmatizing the entire narrative —as a minister, in high position, has recently ventured to do —as a fiction. In a series of startling sermons on the play of the imagination in the sacred writings, the clergyman referred to has put the question—"Why should we think it is inconsistent with a reverence for the Bible as an inspired collection of literature—to think that the Book of Esther, the Book of Ruth, much of the Book of Daniel, and the story of Jonah and the great fish are fiction? It is a matter of no concern whatever spiritually whether we believe a great fish swallowed Jonah or not. No man is better for believing it; no man is worse for not believing it. Nothing in your life or mine depends upon the opinions we entertain on that subject."

Feeling deeply, as I do, upon the subject of Divine Inspiration; believing, as I do, that the honor of God, as well as the destiny of man is staked upon the veracity of His every word; assured as I am, that, if Jonah is fiction, the whole volume of which it forms a part is fiction—more than this, convinced as I am, that the evil wrought by any attack whether open, or more covert upon the integrity of Scripture, is in proportion to the eminence of the man who presumes to shock the common sentiment by making that attack —which, if made within the Church, is calculated to do tenfold more mischief than all the sneers and cavils of acknowledged infidels and enemies outside—I feel called upon, so far as one pulpit at least is concerned, to rebuke and repel it.

Let me invite you again to a review of this remarkable Book, the Book of Jonah, the very exceptional character of which arrests attention and awakens an expectancy of most important spiritual teaching.

"Undoubtedly," said the great Brooklyn preacher, "There are some in this audience who will be disturbed in their faith by the suggestion that the story of Jonah and the Great Fish is a fiction." Precisely—then why disturb their faith? Why breathe the poisonous unholy suggestion?

The question of the *Miracle* lies at the base of the Bible. Prove its miracles false and the foundation is out from under, the superstructure of revelation has fallen.

The Bible is the only Book in the world—claiming to be a Divine Revelation—which professes to rest upon miracles. In other systems, as that of the Zend-Avesta, the Koran, the Book of Mormon, miracles hang upon them and are their appendage. They do not make salvation depend, as the Bible does, on belief in supernatural facts like that of the incarnation of Christ, a miracle without which our redemption were impossible, or that of His resurrection—of which St. Paul says: "If Christ be not risen, if the Miracle be not a fact, then is our preaching vain, and your faith is also vain."

To deny the Miracle then is to deny Revelation. It is to shut God out of His own Book and out of His universe. A God without miracles would be the Miracle of miracles. "It is a superfluous question," says Funcke, "whether God can work miracles, or whether it is necessary to our religious life that we believe in a God who works miracles. For if we have a God who cannot work them, we have a God who is not living, and, if we have a God who is not living, and able to communicate with men, we have no God at all. The question of the Miracle, then, is not secondary, but touches the very heart of religion." Lessing, whom no one could accuse of pietism, said: "He who despoils religion of the things surpassing reason, has *no* religion any more." The infidel Rousseau exclaims: "Can God work miracles? The question is absurd, one would do the man who raises it too much honor to answer him, he should be sent to the madhouse."

Deny the miracle in Jonah, and you deny it everywhere. Says St. Augustine, *Quod aut omnia Divina miracula credenda non sunt, aut hoc, cur non creditur, causa nulla sit*— "Either all Divine miracles are to be rejected, or there is no reason why this one should not be believed." There is nothing more improbable in it than in the splitting of the Red Sea, the falling of the walls of Jericho, or the standing still of the sun and the moon at the mandate of Joshua.

"To my mind," says Kelly, "a miracle, although no doubt it is an exertion of Divine power, and entirely outside the ordinary experience of man, is the worthy intervention of God in a fallen world. It is a seal given to the truth, in the pitiful mercy of God who does not leave a fallen race and lost world to its own remediless ruin. So far, therefore, from miracles being the slightest real difficulty, any one who knows what God is might well expect Him to work them in such a world as this."

Passing from these preliminary observations let me make three points:

I. Christ Himself stands or falls with the Book of Jonah.

II. Jonah in his person and experience is a striking illustration of the Doctrines of Grace.

III. Not only doctrine, but the Practical and experimental in religion are equally conspicuous in this great Missionary Book.

I. Christ Himself stands or falls with the Book of Jonah. This is evident from the fact that He singles out the particular point of greatest difficulty in the Book as the pivotal sign of the genuineness of His claims, and applies to it His own Almighty stamp of authority. In other words, He stakes His Divinity upon the miracle of Jonah's being swallowed and restored by the fish. So that if the Miracle is false, Christ is.

Three times our Lord refers to Jonah in the Gospels, and each time with a singular distinctness. In Matt. XII:39 we read, "Then certain of the Scribes and Pharisees answered, saying, Master, we would see a sign from Thee—*credentials* of Thy Messiahship and Heavenly Commission!" "But He answered and said unto them, An evil and adulterous generation seeketh after a sign; and there shall no sign be given to it, but the sign of the prophet Jonas. For as Jonas was three days and three nights in the whale's belly; so shall the Son of Man be three days and three nights in the heart of the earth. The men of Nineveh shall rise in judgment with this generation and shall condemn it; because they repented at the preaching of Jonas and behold a greater than Jonas is here."

"How are we to explain," says an acute and trenchant writer, "how are we to explain and interpret this language of our Lord in His references to Jonah and to the facts of his history? He calls him Jonah the *prophet*. He speaks of his confinement in the belly of the fish as a *sign* (τὸ σημεῖον) a *real miracle* like His own death and burial. He says he preached in *Nineveh*. He says, the people *repented*, and that their repentance would, *on the judgment day*, condemn the impenitence of the people to whom He Himself was preaching. He says, "Behold, a *Greater than Jonah* is here." What way is there of evading the plain and ordinary meaning of such expressions? What way of preventing, therefore, a direct collision on these points between

THE DOCTRINES OF GRACE 123

the so called higher criticism and the authority of Jesus Christ? Those critics who in explaining this book relegate to the regions of fable, dream or moral fiction, whatever to their natural reason seems improbable, whatever they think *ought not* to have happened, whether it happened or not, are they not really, however they may mean it, attempting to sap the very foundations of Christianity?

See, for a moment, how these critics put the matter. "Can we believe," say they, "that the foundations of a supernatural religion, of a religion taking hold of eternity, can be made to rest upon the absolute historical accuracy of certain alleged material facts? upon facts often trivial, upon facts even preposterous and in which the sharp and merry wits of men have found only what is grotesque and unworthy of God? Shall we believe that a spiritual religion, a religion dealing with the invisible, a religion involving high immortal principles, a religion of holiness, of love, and of internal consciousness can be made to depend, for all that it is, on such trifles, such facts—or rather such fancies—as these?"

This kind of language sounds specious enough, but who cannot see how far away it is from the point? There is, indeed, no question as to the principles of religion. They are of necessity unchangeable and eternal—as high above the facts of history as heaven is above the earth. But then what? We are not saved by principles but by a Person. Principles did not die on the Cross for us, but Jesus Christ, who claims to be the Son of God, did. Who cannot see that, this being so, everything depends, and to the minutest, upon Jesus Christ? If He may be mistaken in His facts, and in a whole continuous chain of them completing an entire chapter of history, thinking, Himself, and asserting that *this, that* and the *other thing* occurred, when the story was nothing other or better than fancy and fable and fiction—in fine, "a historical novel"—where is the *foundation* of our trust? Does it not rest no longer on the Omniscient Son of God, but on an ignorant man and unwise one? upon a man more credulous, more easily imposed upon than are our sagacious and keen-sighted critics to-day?

Or take the only other and darker alternative. If He, *not* mistaken, but knowing and well aware that there was nothing of historical truth in the story, deliberately tells it as true, where again is the *foundation* of our trust? Does it not rest upon an Imposter, a liar, *i. e.*, a deliberate Fraud?

The thing then touches Christ. It *vitally* touches His honesty, His truthfulness, His foresight, His omniscience, His wisdom, His Godhead. *If Jonah falls, Christ falls.* If Christ falls, Christianity falls. "If the FOUNDATIONS BE DESTROYED what can the righteous do?"

II. Not only so, not only does Christ Himself stand or fall with the Book of Jonah, but Jonah, in his person and experience, is a singular and Divinely inspired illustration of the *whole scheme of redemption* involved in the Doctrines of Grace.

The Miracle itself, in Jonah, is not that which distinguishes it as a Book from all others. It is rather the amount and the kind of the miracle. *Other* Books contain miracles, but this one, from beginning to end, is a continuous succession of surprises, providences, miracles and marvels of the most unusual description. What is *more* significant still, is that these marvels—while they appear not necessary to the practical accomplishment of the object in hand—which is to send a man to perform an errand in Nineveh—are, as we closely look at them, found to be,

First—Tremendous proofs of a *Divine* commission and working. To this very day, the entire coast of the Levant from Egypt to Constantinople—including the Grecian Archipelago—abounds with legends, such as the rescue of Andromeda from a sea monster, by Perseus near the rock still pointed out at Joppa. The fable of Hercules swallowed and cast up alive, after three days, by a fish, while laboring to save Hesione the daughter of Laomedon, the King of Troy, and called, for that exploit ‘Ηρακλῆς Τριέσπερος, Hercules of the three nights. The fable of Aia saved from the Dragon or Sea Serpent at Beirut by St. George, together with the emphasis put by all the Mohammedan world on the story of Jonah which occupies the tenth chapter of the Koran, and especially upon the *prayer* of Jonah, which the Mohammedans regard as one of the holiest of all their prayers and frequently use in their devotions.

This, together with the constant recurrence of the picture of Oannes or the Fish-man on the sculptures unearthed at Nineveh, and the Assyrian tradition that this Fish-man was sent to the region of the Euphrates and Tigris to teach the people the knowledge and the fear of God—that he came up from the sea and spake with man's voice the oracles of the Almighty,—

This congeries of myths and legends, evidently suggested by the life and work of Jonah and the impressions left by it, gives grand and solemn confirmation to the fact that God used him in an overwhelming revelation of Himself. But,

Secondly—Not only did God stamp Himself—His Personality, on the whole heathen world—as by no other agency before the coming of the Lord—by Jonah, but He gave, in Jonah, a complete theology in object lessons—including the *depravity* and lost condition of man; his salvation by a *substitute:* the *sovereignty* of God in this work—the power of an *irresistible grace,* and the *final preservation* of all who put their trust in Him.

Let us note in detail.

The *depravity,* or the lost condition of man. Jonah is, no doubt, a child of God, but the "flesh" is in Jonah and that flesh is as *bad* in him as in any man. In the first chapter, we have the working of the flesh in apostasy—we have Adam and Eve represented, after the fall, in the garden. "And Jonah rose up to flee from the presence of the Lord—" "and Adam and his wife hid themselves in the trees of the garden." The essence of all the depravity there is in the world is in fleeing from God—in refusing like Cain, to listen. In doing one's own wilful will and becoming a wanderer. All sins—all recklessness—all falseness—all spiritual indifference and slumber—all sleeping in the stupor of sin are included in one definition—"Fleeing from God—without God and without hope in the world." Jonah was disobedient. God commanded him and he disobeyed God. Jonah was self-willed. He found a ship going to Tarshish. He found it himself. God did not find it for him. It was his own thought—his own project. "God," it is said, "made man upright, but they have found out the knowledge of evil inventions." Jonah was reckless. Having found the ship, "he paid the fare thereof." He said to himself— "Let alone! I will do it, whatever the cost." How many a man has thus said—"I will have it, or her—I will have my own way, if it damns me!"

Jonah deceived the sailors when he paid the fare. His whole life from that moment was a lie; his position, toward God and man, a false one with only one end to it. When Jonah thought of that he ignored it. He sank down in a stupor. He went down into the ship's hold and courted the oblivion of sleep. Vivid type he is of the indifferent unawaked sinner—"dead in trespasses and sins."

But again: The ship's company is saved by one flung overboard and sacrificed for many. Here is a change and Jonah takes a new relation, that of a *substitute*. He becomes the type of our Saviour, both in death and resurrection.

The mariners cry to their gods; they apply to their homemade religion. They cast forth their cargo into the sea. This is like the sinner in a tempest of conviction reforming himself and throwing sin overboard. Not only so but the sailors make strenuous efforts. They do their best to save themselves. They "row hard" to bring their storm tossed ship to land. They toil to the uttermost in their rowing.

No use! They cannot save themselves nor help to save themselves. Jonah must die for them. Another must save them. The grand exchange and substitution is accomplished. Jonah sinks into the belly of hell and the whole ship's company are delivered.

Then, once more: Jonah, in the belly of hell, sees himself lost and puts himself at the *disposal of God*. He learns the Pauline theology in a strange college. Down in the whale's belly he became convinced that it would not be *his* choice but *God's choice* that would save him. If God saw fit to *leave* him, he was gone.

Jonah here changes again; takes the lost sinner's place and lays himself at the foot of God's sovereignty. Salvation is not of Jonah. He sees this, and when he thoroughly sees it, God says to the whale, "Now vomit him up." Jonah is lost as he is in the belly of hell. Salvation *is* of the Lord.

Then again: Salvation is by *irresistible influence*. God moves on the whale to cast Jonah up. Some say, "It was not a whale." They say there are no whales in the Mediterranean. This is untrue. We saw, my wife and I, the skeleton of a whale, more than fifty feet long, at Beirut. The missionaries told us the waves had washed it up on the sands.

If God could make so wonderful a thing as a Jonah, He could make so wonderful a thing as a fish big enough to swallow him—the Scriptures no where say it was a whale—and if He could do *that,* He could move that fish, afterward, to throw Jonah up.

God not only moved on the *fish,* but He moved on the Ninevites. All the preaching in the world in such a case would have amounted to nothing. A man traveling along the streets of New York and crying out: "This city is doomed!" would draw no attention, save as eccentric, save as a fanatic. God moved Nineveh and moved on separate individuals from the King down. He turned them as the rivers of water are turned; He made them willing in the day of His power.

Once more, God taught in Jonah the *eternal preservation* of His own. He preserved Jonah even though a whale swallowed him. He will preserve the soul that trusts in Him, even though the perils of hell are around him—though the jaws of the dragon have seemed to swallow him up. He will preserve the Church within the ribs of His eternal covenant as He did Jonah within the ribs of the great fish and as He did Noah within the timbers of the Ark. He will preserve the Hebrew race. Even though they seem to go down amid the waves of turbulent tumultuating nations and to be lost beneath the sea of history, yet—in their twelve tribes, intact—they shall emerge. They shall be cast up and out again upon the shores of their own land, and Palestine re-peopled shall fulfil the wonderful predictions, not only hinted at in Jonah, but affirmed, with one consent, by all God's prophets.

Not only is Jonah thus indissolubly interwoven with the Gospels in its type of Christ, and with the Epistles of the New Testament in its doctrines; but it is also indissolubly interwoven with the Acts of the Apostles—as being the great Missionary Book of the Old Testament, spreading its Evangel, as it does, from Tarshish in Spain to the banks of

Indus; and with the Apocalypse as pointing to the conversion of both Jew and Gentile in a world reclaimed to God—portrayed in all the glowing scenes of the millennium to come. But

III. The practical and experimental in the Christian life are equally conspicuous in this extraordinary book.

"It displeased Jonah exceedingly"—well now look at it.

This Mission, *first,* was an opposition to Jonah's national prejudices. Nothing is so strong as prejudice—or perhaps as race or religious prejudice. Here both were combined. Israel was to be rejected. She was to be carried into captivity by this very Nineveh; a thought insupportable to a patriotic and God fearing Israelite—and yet to this idolatrous Nineveh—on a mission of blessing—was Jonah sent.

Then *again*: God seemed to falsify Jonah's message. He did not falsify it—for the Nineveh Jonah went to was destroyed—*i. e.,* it was made another and a converted and God-fearing city. It was not a God-fearing city that God would or could destroy.

Moreover, the threat was conditional and Jonah knew it to be conditional. He knew he was not sent to Nineveh to ruin Nineveh but to save her. "This was my saying," he complains—"when I was in my own country—I knew how it would turn out."

Poor Jonah was only a man. He was jealous with a needless jealousy for the honor of God. His country was in danger from this Assyrian power which he had hoped, in spite of hope, was now to be utterly humbled. Above all, his own reputation as a prophet was touched—and we none of us know how far the personal enters into our judgments, to warp us. Jonah had *hoped* while Justice drew the glittering sword; but when mercy sheathed it, and perils thronged the vision of his future, Jonah broke down. He became—for the time—a pessimist. The age was out of joint. The world rushes to chaos. "Everything goes against me," cries Jonah. "Everybody is against me; God himself exposes me to disgrace and disregards my feelings." That is Jonah under the gourd.

Very sad is all this upon the prophet's part, but not so very exceptional. Have you and I my brethren never been displeased and disconcerted by the course things were taking? Have we never spoken a peevish murmuring word—have we never offered an unbelieving prayer.. Have we never seemed to arrive at the bitter end of it when we could not any longer understand God? Or have we never been tempted to think our way would have been better. Have we never tried to mend God's ways, to rectify His providence, to turn the course of things this way or that—after it was manifest that the Great Supreme Ruler had chosen that way and not this? If so, then *we have been Jonah.*

Above all—and here I hope I come nearer, more comfortingly nearer to your experience—have you, amid the reverses and thwartings of life, amid the sighings and the frettings of a wounded spirit—not wilfully rebellious nor consciously revolting against God—have you, with all His children under grievous and not joyous discipline, betaken yourself to the universal curative of prayer? Have you talked with Him about it as Jonah did until the heat and vehemence of your passion died away and in sweet brokenhearted contrition you were willing to justify God and even to sit down and write out the story of your sin, without one word of apology for *yourself* and so leave God right, and yourself forever in the wrong—but filled with an unutterable peace that passes understanding? Then, again, *you have been Jonah.* Then you have found submission to God and trust in God the dearest of all earthly portions and can say—

"He chose this path for me;
No feeble chance, nor hard, relentless fate,
But love, His love, hath placed the footsteps here;
He knew the way was rough and desolate,
Knew how my heart would often sink with fear,
Yet tenderly He whispered, 'Child, I see
 This path is *best* for thee.'"

"He chose this path for me;
Though well He knew sharp thorns would tear my feet,
Knew how the troubles would obstruct the way,
Knew all the hidden dangers I would meet,

Knew how my faith would falter day by day,
And still the whisper echoed, 'Yes, I see
    This path is *best* for thee.' "

"He chose this path for me;
E'en while He knew the fearful midnight gloom
My timid, shrinking soul must travel through;
How towering rocks would oft before me loom,
And phantoms grim would meet the frightened view;
Still comes the whisper, 'My beloved, I see
    This path is *best* for thee.' "

"He chose this path for me;
What need I more? This sweeter truth to know?
That all along these strange, bewildering ways,
O'er rocky steeps, and where dark rivers flow,
His loving arms shall bear me all my days;
A few steps more, and I myself shall see
    This path was BEST for me."

DIFFICULTIES IN THE BIBLE

WORDS FOR THE UNSETTLED IN SOUL

"Yet ye say, The way of the Lord is not equal. Hear now, O house of Israel: is not my way equal? Are not your ways unequal."
—Ezek. xviii:25.

———:o:———

Two principles which we must take with us and always employ in the study of Scripture are these:

1. Direct assertions cannot be invalidated by indirections; the Indicative by a Subjunctive; the positive by an "if."

2. A mystery is not a contradiction. A mystery is a fact which we cannot explain. A contradiction is no fact; it is a statement involving one or more falsehoods; it is a proposition which neutralizes and explodes itself.

The sinner's position is that God's ways are unequal. This is his excuse, or one of his chief excuses, for disobeying God. He brings forward many supposed self-contradictions in the Bible.

I purpose to take up some of these and handle them, as specimens of others, in a very simple and straightforward way. Not that I can, in a short sermon elaborate a complete justification of God; that is a work too broad for any sermon and too broad for man. It is the work of the Supreme and Christ-revealing Spirit. My work is narrow and special: by the Spirit's gracious help, to start the sinner from behind his barricades; to let in daylight and make him think.

What, then, are some of his difficulties if not alleged contradictions?

I. The Bible represents God as omnipotent, and yet asserts there are some things which God cannot do. If God is omnipotent, why does he not abolish hell?

Reply 1st.—Omnipotence does not mean that God can do *everything*, but everything that does not involve a self-contradiction—everything that is an object of power. That a thing should *be* and *not be* at the same moment; that a circle at the same time should be a square; that a creature should be infinite, or a human body everywhere, are self-contradictions, absurdities, and not objects of power.

Reply 2d.—Omnipotence does not mean that God can do the *morally impossible*. A man has power to commit suicide —that is, he can take a razor and draw it across his throat. Any man can do that; physically he has the power. But a good man cannot commit suicide. So a holy God cannot deny Himself—cannot lie—cannot make another God, for these things would be to array Himself against Himself; to commit suicide; to destroy His own perfection.

Reply 3d.—Omnipotence does not mean that God can thwart his own attributes or frustrate His own purposes; that He can do anything contrary to His own Being, character or glory. The omnipotence of God is not what some men picture it, a reckless and irresponsible Almightiness let loose like a wild beast to run careering through the universe. God's omnipotence is a locomotive that runs on straight lines. It is infinite power guided by and under the control of infinite wisdom, infinite justice, infinite truth.

God, though omnipotent, cannot abolish hell. Why? Because His wisdom sees that hell must exist. His justice demands it, and His word is pledged for it. "The soul that sinneth, it shall die." "The wicked shall be turned into hell." Physically, God can do anything that is an object of power. Morally, God can do nothing inconsistent with His own perfection. That is the Bible representation of omnipotence all the way through, and in that representation there is not the hint or shadow of a contradiction.

II. The Bible represents God as loving the world, and as saving the world, and as willing that no man should perish; and yet the same Bible teaches that many are lost, that a remnant are saved, and that "the election hath obtained it while the rest were blinded."

Reply.—There is a difference between God's love of benevolence and God's love of relationship and union. I may have a true love for my neighbors, but I have but one wife. I may love my neighbor's children, but I have a special regard for my own. With a love of benevolence God loves the whole world. Yes, He has a greater love for this world than for any other, and for this race than for any other. My brother, my sister, whoever you are, you belong to the race that God pre-eminently loves; to the race that Jesus died for, and to the race that the Holy Spirit is gathering home to His bosom.

But let us look at the texts that are quoted as pertinent here and read them in the full and exact breadth of their meaning.

John iii:16: "For God so loved the world that He gave His only begotten Son"—for what purpose? To save *individuals*—"That *whosoever believeth in Him* should not perish."

John iii:17: "For God sent not His Son into the world to condemn the world, but that the world, through Him might be saved." Does that text teach Universalism? It does not. It cannot be tortured to teach it. It only teaches that it was not God's intention to perform a work of *condemnation* down here, but a work of *salvation*. The contrast is between these two things. The mission was not to condemn, but to save.

2. Peter iii:9: "Not willing that any should perish, but that all should come to repentance." Here the *willing* spoken of is not active, but passive. The teaching is not that God has willed, actually determined, that not a man shall perish; but the teaching is that God has no desire that any man should perish. If he perishes he perishes of his own self-motion. He gets no push downward from God. "As I live, saith the Lord God, I have no pleasure in the death of him that dieth, but that the wicked turn from his way and live; turn ye, turn ye from your evil ways, for why will ye die, O house of Israel."

God in Ezekiel declares that He takes no pleasure in the death of any man; that he will have nothing to do with it; that if men go to work and destroy themselves they alone must bear the blame and the responsibility. God wills against no man. On the contrary, he has a goodwill toward all. But this is not necessarily an *effective* will. I may think a great deal of a man and yet not choose him for my partner or make him my legatee. God loves the world, but He has chosen His people out of the world. God is the Saviour of all men, in a temporal way, in a conditional way, but especially is He "the Saviour of them that believe,"—1 Tim. iv:10. God wills the salvation of our race. He has given a Gospel for all men. He would have us preach it to all men; but this the *will* of Him that sent Me, the will within the will, "that every one that seeth the Son, and *believeth* on Him, may have everlasting life." Now there is not the hint nor shadow of a contradiction in these two representations. The waters of the Nile belong in a sense to the whole Land of Egypt, but they are effectively, constantly and productively applied to the Delta. So with the love of God. It flows *over* all men; it flows effectively, eternally, productively *into* the hearts of His people.

III. The Bible represents God as holy, and yet guilty of the grossest injustice in punishing us for Adam's sin.

Reply.—God does not do this. God punishes no man for Adam's sin, but for his own sin. In the Bible there is no such representation as this: that God sits upon the throne of judgment and takes men to task for Adam's sin. You cannot find such a representation between the two lids of the Bible. On the contrary, if any sinner can show that he is righteous, that he himself has never sinned, he will never hear anything about Adam. "Yet ye say, why? doth not the son bear the iniquity of the father? When the son hath done that which is lawful and right, and hath kept all my statutes, and hath done them, he shall surely live."—Ezek. xviii:19. If you can square yourself to that text, my brother; if you can show that you have kept all God's statutes; if you can show that you have never had any complicity with Adam in the affair of sin, you have nothing to fear about Adam. Just you get up and show your immaculate purity to God and to the universe, and it will be enough.

But it was unjust to make Adam our federal head.

Reply 1st.—The federal or representative principle runs through the universe. One generation commits another in spite of itself. Our fathers erected the Republic and made us Americans. We cannot help ourselves. They committed us to a republic. We are born republicans by their act, and not monarchists.

Reply 2d. The race must have either stood in a full grown man, with a full-orbed intellect, or stood as babies, each entering his probation in the twilight of self-consciousness, each deciding his destiny before his eyes were half-opened to what it all meant. How much better would that have been? How much more just? But could it not have been some other way? There was no other way. It was either the baby or it was the perfect, well-equipped, all-calculating man—the man who saw and comprehended everything. That man was Adam. He was not deceived. The Scripture says he was not. He knew just what he was about. He did what he did deliberately. Deliberately he wrecked himself and us. Deliberately he murdered his eternal generations. Deliberately he jumped the precipice. Like many another who has loved "not wisely but too well," he would not lose his Eve. He chose her rather than God. He determined he would have her if he went to hell with her.

Reply 3d. If we had not fallen by one man, we could not have been saved by One Man. If we are lost by consenting to Adam, we shall be saved by consenting to Christ. Where is the injustice or the unholiness in all this? Where is the hint or shadow of a contradiction.

IV. The Bible represents God as love, and yet as the author of the most cruel actions. He commanded the Jews to exterminate the Canaanites, and He was so vindictive as to torture and to kill His own Son.

Reply 1st.—God was not cruel in the extermination of the Canaanites unless all sentence against crime is cruel. Turn back and read. You will find that those Canaanites were the Borgias and the Cencis of their time. Their sins were too horrible for description. They were sins that cause the tongue to cleave to the roof of the mouth. They were sins which were eating society through and through like a cancer which must be cut out. God had a right to cut out that cancer. God had the same right to destroy the Canaanites that he had to destroy the Antediluvians or Sodom. Again, God had a perfect right to select what executioners

He pleased. He selected the Jews. He guarded against any personal feeling on their part by making their function strictly official. He raised the whole transaction to the platform, and the dignity, and the solemnity of law. And how else could God have met this case more wisely or more holily, or how could He have stamped more deeply or more widely on the Jews and on the world at large the salutary sense of His justice?

Reply 2d.—The answer in reference to the Lord Jesus Christ is so easy and obvious that nothing but a wilfully and awfully perverse mind could have missed it.

It was not a vindictive and blood-thirsty spirit in God which led Him to seek the death of His Son as a substitute. God's justice must punish sin. That is an eternal *must* in God. To find fault with it is to find fault—shall I say with the nature of things? I must go higher, and say with the nature of God. What would a God be without justice, and what would a justice be that did not punish sin.

Beside this the universe demanded the punishment of sin. When I was a boy the entire population of Western New York was shocked by the murder of the Van Nest family. I shall never forget the impression. In the dark night, a negro knocked at the door of a farmer's house upon the margin of Owasco Lake. The wife and mother who came to the door was felled by a blow of a bludgeon. The murderer went through the house and put each member of the family to death. He cut their throats or stunned them, and then killed them. When the outrage was known the whole community was up in arms. It was all that the police could do to keep men from lynching that negro. Not only was the law against him, but the public sentiment, with its ten thousand tongues, which echoed and confirmed it. So in the case of the Atonement. The universe, as well as God, demands satisfaction. Let it be seen that God does not intend to punish sin—that He is going to let the brigands and assassins of his moral government run loose—and, up and out from every holy conscience there will come a cry for blood—a cry which gathering volume and momentum as it rolls, will fill creation with anarchic and incessant thunders.

God knew that it was *unsafe,* as well as impossible, to forgive sin without a satisfaction. For this reason it was that

"He spared not His own Son, but delivered Him up for us all," for us who believe. Where in all this is there any element of cruelty. Where is there any invalidation of love? Why, *"herein is love,* not that we loved God, but that He loved us and sent His Son to be a propitiation for our sins."

Not the hint or the shadow of a contradiction is there here.

V. The Bible says that Christ died for all men, and yet again it says that He died for only a part.

Reply 1.—The Bible represents that Christ died for *this world* and no other—for mankind as a *race,* and not angels.

Reply 2d.—The Bible represents that Christ died for all men to secure for them temporal blessings. Without the Cross as a breakwater, death would at once surge over and swamp all our millions.

Reply 3d.—The Bible represents that Christ purchases the Holy Spirit in His ordinary influences for all men, and the Gospel for masses and nations.

Reply 4th.—The Bible represents that Christ died for all men *provided they will accept.* In this sense no man perishes for lack of an atonement. If he perishes he perishes for lack of trusting, not for lack of Christ.

Now right along inside of these representations the Bible constantly affirms that Christ died *savingly* and *efficiently* for His people, His Church, His sheep; and that He is the Saviour of His body, and that His atonement and His intercession are not for the world, but as He Himself says, "I pray not for the world but for them which thou hast given me, for they are thine."

But in John i:29 He is called "the Lamb of God that taketh away the sin of the world." Yes, and so He is—the Sin-Taker for the world, *if they will have Him.*

In John xii:32 it is said: "And I, if I be lifted up, will draw all men to me. Reply.—The word "men" is not in the original; it is an interpolation. The true translation is, "And I, if I be lifted up, will draw all *mine* to me."

I. Tim. ii:6, "Who gave Himself a ransom for all to be testified in due time." Precisely—who the "all" are *will be testified in due time,* by the call of the Spirit, when the books shall be opened.

Heb. ii:9, "He tasted death for every man." Reply.—The word "man" is not in the Greek; it is an interpolation. The true translation must be gathered from the context. The Apostle is speaking of the Eternal Son saving the sons. He goes on, therefore, to say: "He tasted death *for every one of them;* for it became Him, for whom are all things, and by whom are all things, in bringing *many sons* to glory to make the Captain of *their* salvation perfect."

The true doctrine of the Atonement is that Christ is offered to all men; that he dies in the midst of men as a substitute; that he dies for His people; and that all who hear His Gospel and trust in Him are His people, and are from that instant eternally saved. Now what hint or shadow, or faintest trace of contradiction is there here?

VI. The Bible says that the believer is everlastingly saved, and yet that he can fall from grace.

Reply 1.—The Bible does not say that he can fall *out of grace,* if it did God would deny himself, there would be a flat contradiction and we should be puzzled indeed what to reply. What the Bible does say is that the Galatians under their Judaizing teachers had abandoned the ground of free justification on which they had stood. In taking up the old principle of circumcision they had dropped upon a lower platform and fallen back from the principle of grace. That is what the Bible says. That is exactly what it says. Wrest, and twist, and torture the Greek as you please, you can make nothing else of it.

Reply 2.—The Bible statements about everlasting life are positive, and positive assertions cannot be shaken by any mere hypotheses. In John x:26, our Saviour directly and explicitly asserts this doctrine. "Ye believe not," He says, "because ye are not of my sheep." That is going to the root of the matter. But who are the sheep? "My sheep hear my voice, and I know them and they follow Me. And I give unto them eternal life and *they shall never perish* (literally they shall never be able to destroy themselves; to vitiate the grace that is in them), neither shall any man pluck them out of my hand; and even if this could be," He goes on to say, "If any could pluck them out of my hand, there is a hand outside of mine; My Father which gave them Me is greater than all: and no man is able to pluck them out of My Father's hand, *I and My Father,* as to this eternal covenant, *are one."*

But does not the Apostle say in Heb. vi:4, "It is impossible for those who were once enlightened and have tasted of the heavenly gift and were made partakers of the Holy Ghost and have tasted the good word of God, and the powers of the world to come; if they shall fall away, to renew them again to repentance?"

Reply 1st.—This is a mere hypothesis, *"If they shall fall away,"* "if,"—the graceless will fall away, but God provides for the "if" in the case of His true people as He says in Ps. xxxvii:31, "None of their steps shall slide."

Reply 2d.—The text taken absolutely asserts the impossibility of any renewal at all. So that if it means to say a man can fall from actual grace, it means to say he cannot be renewed again. According to such an interpretation there is no hope for any backslider. Once fallen, he is doomed; it is hopeless to preach to him.

Reply 3d.—The text says nothing about *actual* grace but only about certain hopeful but delusive signs of it. A man may be *"enlightened"* as to the doctrine; he may *"taste of the heavenly gift"*—that is, have some speculative superficial knowledge of, and fancied love for Christ—a thing very different from "eating His flesh and drinking His blood by a true and internal reception of Him; again he may be a *"partaker of the Holy Ghost"* in His common, external and even powerful influences—as many a man has been greatly moved and even brought to a profession of faith in a time of revival; again he may go further and *"taste the good word of God"* and "anon with joy receive it, all the while, having no life in himself; he may even proceed so far as to show great gifts and "work miracles" like Judas by the *"powers of the world to come."* All this may be true of him and yet he may afterward wilfully and knowingly and deliberately deny and reject the Lord Jesus Christ and commit the unpardonable sin from which there is no renewal. It is no common backsliding, no fall like that of Peter which is here intended, but it is such an apostasy as that of the man who once knowing and professing the truth, deliberately and in the face of full light denies rejects and opposes it, trampling the Blood of Christ beneath his feet—"crucifying to himself the Son of God afresh and putting Him to an open shame." The persons spoken of, then, are not, were not, and never will be in grace, for nothing is more certain than that a man may share all the external things spoken of and yet be a stranger to the reality of religion.

Reply 4th.—The apostle explains himself when he adds that, though thus solemnly warning them, he is "persuaded better things of them and things which, $\dot{\epsilon}\chi\acute{o}\mu\epsilon\nu\alpha$ have in them or involve *salvation*," as the things before mentioned do not. Again, he says that those of whom he has been speaking are fruitless persons, earth which bears thorns and briars and so is rejected, and is nigh unto cursing whose end is to be burned." In contrast with this, those to whom he writes are commended for their work and labor of love which God is not unrighteous to forget.

Reply 5th.—The doctrine (see verses 16 to 20), is that men fall not from grace but from the *lack* of it. That true grace can never fail because of two immutable things,—1st, the Promise of God to keep His people, and 2d, His Oath in which it is impossible for God to lie, or prove false to those who have fled to and found refuge in His word of His promise on which He has caused us to hope.

But does not St. Paul say in I Cor. iv:27, "Lest that by any means, when I have preached to others I myself should be a castaway?"

Reply 1st.—The word *adokimos,* translated "castaway," means "disapproved of; cast aside." It refers to the Apostle's official position. If unfaithful he would be set aside. The Lord would not use him for conversions any more.

Reply 2d.—The Apostle says, "Lest having *preached* to others, I myself," &c. Many preach to others who are lost. The Apostle might perhaps compare his case with theirs. To imagine this is to distort and falsify the language, but even then what St. Paul never said and could not say was this, "Lest being born again I should be lost."

Objection.—If this be so, why does the Saviour say in John viii:31, "If ye *continue* in my word, then are ye my

THE DOCTRINES OF GRACE

disciples, indeed, and ye shall know the truth, and the truth shall make you free?" Again, "He that *endureth* to the end shall be saved."

Reply.—As to the *continuing*. The context shows that these people were *not His disciples at all*. They did not "know the truth." They had not been *made free*. We are talking about true Christians falling from grace. The text therefore, is irrelevant.

As to the *enduring*. God saves men through the will, and therefore He exhorts them. First He works in them to will, and after that they are able to will, and must will, and must be stirred up to it. Hence while salvation as a matter of fact is assured, we are all through the Bible addressed in such a way as makes us feel our personal responsibility. Thus in I. John, ii:27 we have the positive assertion "Ye *shall* abide in Him;" but this is followed in the next sentence by the exhortation, "And *now* abide in Him!" That is, "God's will is for you; let your wills work with God's. You are saved; therefore walk as saved men, not presumptiously, but cautiously, and in the fear of God."

Objection.—"Destroy not him with thy meat for whom Christ died." Reply.—I, a saved soul, may act in such a way as tends to the destruction of another saved soul. God will prevent the catastrophe. He is pledged to prevent it; but I am guilty all the same, and I must be made to feel that. Here is the place for exhortation, for warning, for reproof. I am talked to as if I did the whole thing; for while God saves us he does it not by destroying our responsibility, rather by emphasizing and enlarging it. Is there a hint or shadow of a contradiction in all this? Mystery, at every point, we admit; but we deny contradiction.

VII. The Bible says that men can come to Christ, and it says in the most unequivocal terms (John vi:44) that they cannot.

Reply 1st.—The Bible nowhere says that the natural man, unaided and undrawn, can come to Christ. In all the Scripture there is not one *indicative* assertion of free-will. All invitations are "if," "if," "if." These assert no ability. To tell a man that he may have a book if he pays $5 is not to give him $5. It is only saying he may have it "if."

Reply 2d.—"If thou wilt" shows us the difference between the *Law* and the *Gospel*. The Law says, "Do it;" the Gospel, *"I will do it for you."* The Law says, *"If,"* the Gospel says, *"It is done."* The Old Testament set before us a requirement and a reward, with a chasm between them; the Gospel fills the chasm—it fills it with Christ and His cross.

Reply 3d.—"If thou wilt" teaches us what we ought to do in order to convince us how helpless we are. The object of the *if* is by showing what we ought to do and cannot do, to raise the question, How are we to do it? This brings in Christ.

Reply 4.—While we cannot come to Christ unaided, we *can* come helped by the Holy Spirit; and if we simply lean upon His help, we cannot miss the mark. The point of the thing is something like this. A father has a conceited son. The boy has an immense notion of his own ability. "Very well," says the father, "Roll that stone up the hill yonder." The boy puts his shoulder to the stone and finds he cannot start it. "Roll it up the hill," says the father, "and I will give you a $10 bill." The boy tugs, and tugs, and tugs until he exhausts himself. "Now, when you are ready to confess that you cannot do it yourself; when you are ready to look to me to do it for you," says the father, "I will roll the stone up the hill and give you the $10 beside." The boy with his shoulder to the stone is the Law. The boy standing aside, looking to the father to do it and pocketing the $10 bill, is the Gospel, "for what the Law could not do, in that it was weak through the flesh, God sending His own Son in the likeness of sinful flesh, and for sin, has done in the Gospel."—Rom. viii:3. In all this there is no hint, nor shadow, nor trace of contradiction.

Now what is the outcome, what the resultant, of our work?

1. A line of light runs through the Bible from Genesis to Revelation.

2. This line of light bears down upon the unconverted conscience.

3. This line of light, my unconverted brother, fixes your eternal destiny. You are in that spot of light and cannot get out of it. It burns upon you like a sun-glass.

That turns the tables. It is not God whose ways are unequal, but the sinner whose ways are unequal. I thought so all along. I thought the contradiction was not in the Book, but *in the man*. Sinner! you must break down. You must see yourself utterly vile. You must renounce all your own strength, all your own imaginations, and, prostrate in the dust, you must look up and out to Christ for everything. The instant you do that, quick as the lifting of an eyelash, you are saved. My brother, are you willing now to look to Jesus? Does God make you willing? Oh, then, dear brother, you are saved; you are in grace; give God the glory!

ALMIGHTY GOD, MAKE THINE ETERNAL TRUTH THY SPIRIT'S DEMONSTRATION AND RESISTLESS POWER, FOR JESUS' SAKE, WHO SEALED IT WITH HIS BLOOD.

THE BONDAGE OF THE WILL

Rom. ix:16

"So then it is not of him that willeth, nor of him that runneth, but of God that sheweth mercy."

There are but two religions upon earth. One, that which centers in the dogma of Free-Will; the other that which springs from the Divine Election. One which says, "Salvation is of self-movement;" the other, "Salvation is of the Lord!"

These two religions are two different systems. One metaphysical, which goes to philosophy for its reasons and argues from consciousness and from the nature of things—this system, brought within the circle and the influence of Christianity, does not refuse the Scripture, but evades those parts of Scripture which it cannot seem to subordinate, and of which it cannot make use. The other system stands on Scripture only, and argues from the truth of revelation—from the scope and details of the Book—from facts which have been witnessed by a competent authority, the Holy Ghost. This system, when brought within the circle and the influence of human argument, does not necessarily refuse reason, but subordinates reason, and regards the "If?" of reason, where God speaks, as blasphemy.

These two systems in the Church have been called by different names—Augustinianism and Pelagianism; Calvinism and Arminianism; the Old and New School. With every spiritual crisis, side by side, these rival systems emerge—a bridgeless gulf between them, however names may change.

The one system, were it unopposed, would take its point of departure from God, and from him would argue down the lines of sovereignty, of justice and grace. But, confronted by the other system, whose starting-point is man and Nature, and the so-called shifting "consciousness," the battle-ground becomes that of the human will and of its freedom—Whether the will, in man, is free in such a sense as makes him practically independent, not of God alone, but of himself; of his own nature, character and personality behind it; whether the Will, unfettered, is a power of self-betrayal, self-antagonism, self-reverse; something which flies, or *may* fly, in the man's own face, in spite of him: or, Whether the Will, in man, is but a *faculty among the faculties,* linked to the other faculties, and controlled in movement and in bent by the nature and bent of the man?

What is the Will in man? The soul, itself a trinity, has three great primal powers—the Intellect, or power of seeing; the Affections, or power of feeling; and the Will, or power of volition.

The Will, then, is the faculty or power of willing. Is it an independent, self-determinating power?—*i. e.,* does the Will stand apart from the other great faculties or powers of the soul, *a man within a man,* who can reverse the man and fly against the man and split him into segments, as a glass snake breaks in pieces?

Or, is the Will connected with the other faculties, as the tail of the serpent is with his body, and that again with his head, so that where the head goes, the whole creature goes, and, as a man *thinketh* in his *heart,* so is he? First thought, then heart (desire or aversion), and then act. Is it this way, the dog wags the tail? Or, is it the Will, the tail, wags the dog?

Is the Will the first and chief thing in the man, or is it the last thing—to be kept subordinate, and in its place beneath the other faculties?—and, is the true philosophy of moral action and its process that of Gen. iii:6: "And when the woman saw that the tree was good for food" [sense-perception, intelligence], "and a tree to be desired" [affections], "she took and ate thereof" [the will.]

The latter we affirm because of the statements of Scripture.

But, before coming to these, that we may cut through all vagueness and mystification, straight to the root of the matter, and reach a fair and honest statement of the question, let us premise a few things by way of clearing the ground.

Man is a free agent; but man has not a free will. Man is, therefore, responsible; yet he is impotent. Upon this seeming paradox, but changeless fact, is built the scheme of grace.

The *man* is free, but his *will* is not free. Liberty or freedom from coercion is one thing; ability or power from within is another. All the Reformed Confessions unite on this point. To make it, Luther, in his *"De Servo Arbitrio,"* contends; to make it, Augustine, in his *"De Gratia et Arbitrio,"* contends; to make it, St. Paul, in all his Epistles, contends; to make it, the whole Bible, from cover to cover, is directed. The Bible everywhere holds man responsible, yet everywhere it strips the fallen creature of all spiritual power; writes death upon him; shuts him up, like Nicodemus, to new birth—like Lazarus, to resurrection; asserts that it is not of him that willeth, nor of him that runneth, but of God that showeth mercy"; excludes all boasting and gives all the glory to God.

This being so, the distinction between free agency and free will assumes vital importance, and calls for emphatic assertion. Man is a free agent because unforced from without; he does as he pleases, always as he pleases, only as he pleases; he is therefore responsible. But man has not a free will because he is bound together within—because his judgment moves his desires, and his desires his volitions, just as steam moves the piston and the piston the wheel. While, therefore, man does as he pleases, he pleases and can please only one way. He does as he pleases, but he cannot please against his whole nature—against the unity, tendency, strain of his nature. His nature binds him; if a fallen nature, downward. This nature he cannot reverse. He cannot renew his own will, change his own heart, nor regenerate his bad nature. While therefore, he is free, so far as forces outside are concerned, his will is not free but is bound by the strain of his nature. It is still "the carnal mind" that *will* not—the "enmity" that *"cannot* please God."

An illustration occurs from the hand. It is simple, but perhaps may be helpful. A man is free to use his hand. The *man* is free, but the *hand* is not free; the arm and the muscles control it. The hand is the slave of the muscle, and acts as the muscle compels. In like manner, man is free to use his will, and is therefore always a free agent;

THE DOCTRINES OF GRACE

but the will itself is not free. It is controlled by the affections, which are evil and earthly and sensual, and these again are controlled by the understanding and judgment, which call evil good and which are perverted, blinded, deluded, by the god of this world.

Another illustration is in point—Niagara! The water is free. No one is forcing it. No one is taking up bucketfuls and pouring them over the falls. The water is *unforced from without,* but it forces itself. Each drop pushes another, and so, while Niagara is free and rejoices and leaps in its freedom, the drops are not free, nor can Niagara roll itself backward. Niagara goes down, is bound to go down, and cannot go up.

That is how the Bible puts the impotence of fallen man. Free *to* sin, but free *from* holiness—helpless toward God, the volume, river, trend and tendency of his nature is down. "As a fountain casteth out her waters," says Jeremiah, "so we cast out our wickedness." "Can a fig tree bear olive berries?" Who can bring a clean thing out of an unclean? Can free will do it? Can any thing or creature do it? No! not one.

Man *will not,* because it is not in him to will; he is stunted, and set in a fallen direction; and man *cannot,* because an evil eye affects the heart, and a deceived heart turns him aside, ever aside, from the mark of the prize of God's calling. Man's inability is, therefore, total, innate, ineradicable by any self-help or self-motion, by any twisting, effort, or desire of Nature. Man can no more turn to God than the dead can sit up in their coffins. He can no more originate a right desire than he can create a universe. God and God the Holy Ghost alone, by sovereign, special interference, calls dead sinners to life, and "creates within them the desires of their hearts"—the first faint fluttering of a breath toward holiness.

Such is the representation of the Bondage of the Will, in perfect harmony with Free Agency, which the Bible furnishes, and for which we are bound to contend. It is readily granted, however, that such a notion of things would not and could not occur to man of himself. It is as much beyond his conception as the stars beyond his touch, and when revealed, the first effect is to bewilder, dazzle and confound.

It is readily granted that God's thoughts on this subject are higher than our thoughts—that such a notion of things would not and could not occur to the unregenerate consciousness (for the natural man receiveth not the things of the Spirit of God), but only to the consciousness which has become Christian, and more—not always instantly to that; but slowly and by degrees through the teaching and interpretations of the Spirit. Witness the difference between Whitefield converted suddenly, consciously by force, and the gradual experience of Dr. Scott, the commentator, who began a radical, intense Arminian and ended in a full surrender to the Doctrines of Free Grace.

Suppose I have fallen into the water and am blindly struggling and frantically beating with my arms. All my efforts only serve more surely to sink me. I go down—again—the third time. I have lost consciousness. When I come to, I find myself upon the river bank. I look at the water and I say: "Bravo! I have done well. How I must have struggled! That last stroke did the work and landed me safe on the shore." I *say* this, but I am not satisfied. A person approaches. He is dripping with water. He says: "You were gone! I saw you go down the last time, and I dived under and saved you!" I think it over and I say: "That sounds like fact, like common sense; it seems the only satisfying explanation"; yet consciousness does not help me. I have no recollection of rescue by force and from outside. I must take it on trust.

There are three conditions of the Will.

1. That of holiness fixed and confirmed in holiness. That is the will of God, of Christ incarnate, and of the holy angels. *Non posse peccare*, as Augustine says: "Who cannot sin."

2. That of holiness on trial, unconfirmed, and therefore mutable. That of Lucifer, who fell by vanity; whose eye was caught by self-reflection. That of innocent Adam in Eden. *Posse non peccare*—Able not to sin, but might.

3. The *fallen* will. Unholy, free from holiness. *Non posse non peccare*—"Unable not to sin; sin's helpless slave." This third condition, of the *fallen* will, we argue from the

Scripture. And the arguments to which we shall confine ourselves are five.

(1.) *Direct and plain assertion.* "When we were yet *without strength*, in due time Christ died for the ungodly." "No man *can* come unto Me except the Father which hath sent Me draw him." "Therefore said I unto you that no man can come to Me, except it were *given* him of my Father." "It is the Spirit that quickeneth, *the flesh profiteth nothing.*" "Because the carnal mind is enmity against God; for it is not subject unto the law of God, neither indeed *can be.*" "That which is born of the flesh is *flesh,* and that which is born of the Spirit is spirit." "Which were born not of the will of the flesh, *nor of the will of man,* but of God." "So then, it is *not of him that willeth,* nor of him that runneth, but of God that showeth mercy." "To *will* is present with me" [*i. e.,* the Faculty of Will], "but how to *perform* that which is good" [the power], "I find not." These few texts, taken from hundreds equally peremptory, must suffice for this argument.

(2.) The Bondage of the Will is not only positively and plainly asserted in the Scripture, but it is everywhere *implied*.

It is implied in regeneration. A man comes into this world passive, without either his own act or consciousness, so does he enter the Kingdom of God. It is either this, or we deny the New Birth, and teach the nonsense of self-procreation.

Again: If any man be in Christ, he is a καινὴ κτίσις (new creation). This carries us right back to the first creation, from nothing, and to the infusion into us of something which was not in us before, but now can never be absent. Call it *"Christ* in us," or a *"seed,"* or the *"spirit* born of the Spirit," or call it what you will; it is a fact that cannot be gainsaid. Creation is an object of power.

Again: "You who were *dead* hath He quickened." Is not resurrection an object of power?

Again: Because faith is said to be "the gift of God," and a man takes a gift from outside. Faith is the current of the Divine life, running through the new-born, which is the river of Throne-water, the impetus and energy of God.

And once more: The description of the work of the Spirit as the interposition and impingement of Omnipotence—"Thy people shall be willing in the day of *Thy power.*"

(3.) Add to these assertions and implications, *illustrations;* as, for instance, the turning back of water which cannot run up-hill, nor rise above its own level. "Turn again our captivity as the streams of the South." "All my *fresh* springs are in Thee."

Take again Ezekiel's Vision of the Dry Bones—"very dry"—"no flesh on them." The question is: "Can these bones live?" Free-will says, "Certainly. It is a mockery to say to them, 'Hear the Word of the Lord,' unless they can hear it." But Inspiration answers not so, "Son of man, cry!" "Cry, 'Come from the four winds, O Breath and breathe upon these slain that they *may* live.'"

Ah! "Lazarus Come Forth!" *gives* the Free choice to a dead man and unwraps the cerements of Will, as it proclaims the fiat, "Loose him and let him go!" For, if the Son shall make you free, ye shall be free indeed. Ah! "Stretch forth thy hand!" brings in the miracle of willingness to venture, as it does the miracle of power, enabling the soul paralyzed and conscious of its helplessness to cry, *Da quod jubes, et jube quod vis!*—"Give, only give what Thou commandest, and then command what Thou wilt."

These and all miracles proclaim aloud, by physical expression, the momentous *moral* fact. Can blindness make itself to see? Can deafness unstop its own ears? dumbness its own lips? Can palsy leap and leprosy exude its loathsome virus? Then may the Will work backward, revolutionize itself, fling off contagion wandering through our crooked veins, and, tearing from itself the poisoned shirt of Nessus, speak the emancipating edict—"I will! Self, be clean!"

(4.) The Scripture doctrine, thus asserted, and implied and illustrated, gathers in the *Scope of Revelation*. All other doctrines hang upon and confirm it. What is Election but God choosing, because we cannot choose? What is Regeneration but God quickening the dead who cannot stir? What is Perseverance but God carrying on a work which

He has begun, where *man,* beginning must infallibly break down?

(5.) To these arguments from Scripture let us add, and finally, *the utter absence of any Scriptural authority for the assertion that the Will is free;* or that power must equal obligation, or that any unregenerate man can will aught whatever in the direction of God, or aught whatsoever but sin.

Surely, if the ground of obligation be ability, we have a right to expect the Scripture to say so. Instead of this it says the other thing, and says it every time, and nowhere, in a single instance, contradicts itself. Its uniform refrain, from Genesis to Revelation is—"Every imagination of the thought is evil"—"no man can come to Me except the Father draw." Free-will can do nothing without special grace and an effectual call.

But, do not exhortations and commands take our ability for granted? And when God says "Do a thing," does it not imply that we *can?*

It does not, for

1. Direct assertions cannot be invalidated by mere *in*directions—the Indicative by a Subjunctive; the positive by an "if." Saying "Stretch forth thy hand" does not imply, "Paralysis *can* stretch it." Saying "Ye will not come to Me," does not imply "You can *will* to come to Me." The fact is just the opposite. The diseased will is the trouble. "Ye cannot *will.*"

This is splendidly argued by Luther in his Diatribe against Erasmus. "If thou wilt equal Virgil, my Maevius, thou must sing a more exalted strain. Alas! Maevius cannot."

2. And again: the dogma "Power equals Obligation" proves too much. I ought to keep the commandments, therefore I can; therefore perfection is possible; therefore Sisyphus rolls his stone to the top of the mountain; therefore I can climb a Sinai all aflame, and which not even a beast, stupid as *he* is, would think to touch.

The importance of the doctrine of Inability is thus seen and solemnized from the fact that the whole Bible is directed—the strength of the Holy Ghost, if one may so say, gathered up to prove it—to show that man can neither save himself, nor help to do it—can neither turn himself, nor help to do it; that common grace, however it may move on men is not sufficient; that while men have power downward, they have no power upward; that a fallen creature can only keep falling; and that if ever men turn to God, it must be by God's turning them, and if ever they are willing, it must be because *made* willing in the day of sovereign and Almighty power.

The importance of the doctrine of Inability is further seen and solemnized from the fact that without it men will never cease their fleshly efforts and their fleshly willings and their fleshly vows, and simply trust on Christ. Sisyphus must quit, and let Another roll that stone. Worldly Wiseman must fly from Sinai to Golgotha.

A sense of helplessness, absolute, utter, is the first requisite to any sound conversion, and this sense of helplessness is nothing more nor less, nor other, than old-fashioned *conviction of sin.*

THE DOCTRINE OF GRACE

"For the grace of God that bringeth salvation hath appeared unto all men teaching us that denying ungodliness and worldly lusts, we should live soberly, righteously, and godly in this present world."—Titus ii:11, 12.

Practical Christianity has for its ground and motive doctrinal Christianity. It is principle, straight through, that is to sustain men and move men according to God. It is principle, not emotion, not impulse. That is the root-thought of the Epistle to Titus. St. Paul speaks first, in the first chapter, of church order and holiness in the church—then he speaks, in the second chapter, of family order and holiness in the family—then he speaks, in the third chapter, of social order and holiness in our relation to the world. But each of these three phases of conduct is described as the outcome of a great truth clearly known and quietly taken for granted, namely, that of our personal relation to God—a relation which is all that the affections can desire, and which never changes, because it depends entirely and forever upon what God is, whose self-consistency is perfect.

For the grace of God which *bringeth* salvation, which comes down from heaven with it, which does not look for righteousness from us but gives it, hath appeared to all men, teaching us that denying ungodliness and worldly lusts, we should live soberly, righteously and godly in this present world.

In the exposition of these words, according to the line of apostolic thought, I wish to follow three inquiries:

I. What is the Doctrine of Grace?
II. How this Doctrine hath appeared unto all men.
III. Its practical effect.

I. What is the Doctrine of Grace?

The word grace means favor to the ill-deserving; the doctrine of grace then must mean that system of truth which has for its foundation *the ill-desert of sinners* before God.

Grace is something which must always come in after justice. It is something entirely supplementary to any work of righteousness—something over and above. It is imperative that we should see this, otherwise we can have no proper conception of the plan of redemption. So long as we imagine that God has to deal with innocent creatures or with creatures who have a claim upon Him, who have not already fallen under His justice, we shall be utterly non-plussed and unable to receive the first and simplest propositions of the Gospel. The fact is that, before grace can come in, the bottom must be knocked out from under man, and he must be let down to the moral status of a devil. The level on which we stand, my brethren, is precisely that of fallen spirits. The only difference between unregenerate man and devils is this, that man has a body and devils have not. Man has the *nature* of Satan—"Ye are of your father the devil." Man is as blind as Satan—"Ye were sometimes darkness." Man is as wilful as Satan—"The lusts of your father ye will do." Man is led and energized by Satan—"The spirit that now worketh in the children of disobedience." Lost man is a lost spirit, and God has a right to deal with him as He deals with lost spirits. That is the fundamental proposition of grace.

Well, now: How has God dealt with lost spirits? He has condemned them. He has cast them out of His presence. He has doomed them to hell. Let us, in imagination, lift the cover from hell. What do we see there? We see millions of once glorious creatures writhing in torments. We see them committed to a destiny which must grow worse and worse, and which is unchangeable. Forever and forever each single devil must suffer. Not one can ever escape. That is justice. It is the stern and iron reign of law.

What do we say of that? How do we feel about it? We say it is right. We acquiesce. I never yet heard any man complain of God, for treating the devils as a criminal class. I never yet heard of a man who sat down and wept over devils, because of what they had to suffer. God has punished devils and He is going to punish them. He is going to spend the exhaustless powers of retribution on their immortality—to pour wrath on them to the uttermost.

Now, suppose God were to determine to bring in a salvation for the devils. He is not going to do it. Their affairs are closed up. Righteousness with them has reached its everlasting finality...... But, for the sake of illustrating the point before us, let us suppose a salvation for devils. Must it necessarily be for all devils? Why? Why must God save *all* if He saves any? Why has God no option? Why has He less liberty than I have, when to one of two street beggars I give a dime and to another nothing? If God is free at the first step, why is He not free at each succeeding step? If not, where does He lose His freedom? If He may save or not save, may He not save few or many—one or ten thousand. I would like to sharpen emphasis upon this point. I have no desire to evade it, but rather to pursue it and to corner it—to compel a categorical reply.

Is God bound to save everything that sins and suffers? No, for

1st. He does not do it. We see unrelieved suffering all around us.

2. God's justice will not let Him do it. There is an eternal principle in God which must treat sin as sin deserves.

God, then, is free to save or not to save. His will is entirely untrammelled. Suppose He says, "I will save," still has He power over His own will to determine how many; or else from the moment of becoming a Saviour He uncrowns Himself as a God.

In the case before us, God might come down and save certain, we will say, eight devils, while He left the others just where they were. Imagine this and what would be the effect? Why, in the case of the majority they would continue to get what they have been getting—what they were sentenced to, what they deserve. In them God and His justice are glorified. In the case of the others, of the eight, the thing done would be supplementary. It would not be necessary; it would not be expected; it would not be called for. It would therefore be a simple and unmixed gratuity, and, to those benefited, this gratuity would be the spring and cumulating motive of all possible eternal gratitude and praise.

Now this illustration of the devils is the exact fact with reference to fallen man. Our salvation is built upon the condemnation of devils, into which we also have fallen. But in our case, God makes a difference. After the sentence has been pronounced—after the gallows-tree has been erected—after the drop has been sprung, God brings in a new thing—a thing which has entered no thought, which is beyond a creatural imagination, and which circulates throughout all heavenly regions and throughout all holy and angelic populations an overwhelming, yet blissful, surprise.

That thing which God brings in is grace. Eternal grace which contemplates a ruined, guilty, utterly corrupt and helpless sinner—a collapse in sinnership—a synocope of sin. Grace is a provision for men who are so fallen that they cannot lift the axe of justice—so corrupt that they cannot change their own natures—so averse to God that they cannot turn to Him—so blind that they cannot see Him—so deaf that they cannot hear Him and so dead that He Himself must open their graves and then lift them into resurrection.

Grace then is not like justice, a necessary attribute in God. It is an optional attribute, and if optional includes

1st. As its first element *an everlasting choice*. Suppose there *were* no choice. Suppose God had precipitated our whole race to death, as He did angels, from the moment that they sinned. God might have done this. It would have been no excess of severity. It would have been justice, only justice still achieving its untarnished if appalling triumphs. But *what then?* Why then a race drops out—a link, the human is lost to the universe—a whole intelligent nature made capable of the eternal enjoyment of God comes short of that for which it came into existence. What then? Why then Satan conquers and stalks over the battle-field the undisputed monarch of a subjugated world. What then? Why then the law which was given, first of all, not that men should suffer by its penalty, but that God should be glorified by its fulfilment, is never complied with. Thus justice, in the destruction of our race would triumph—but in the defeat of all the other perfections of God.

Suppose the *opposite*—that God had saved *all men*. What then?

Why then there is the obliteration of justice. To all eternity it can never be made to appear that we did really deserve to die. In spite of the cross we ourselves should doubt it—angels would doubt it. The universe would doubt it. Some men must die to set that doubt at rest. Over the grave of some there must go forth the announcement, in terms at once decisive and incontrovertible, that "all have sinned and come short of the glory of God," and that those who are saved "were by nature the children of wrath even as others." Without this there will be a race of sinners, no individual of whom ever gets his personal ill-deserts, or ever believes that he had any! Without this there will be one world afloat among the worlds which flings a jarring discord over all the harp-strings of the heavenly minstrelsy; which sports in a derisive freedom; and which laughs aloud at righteousness.

But suppose a third thing. Suppose justice and mercy combined. Suppose that when all deserve condemnation, and all are seen to deserve it, some are saved—a multitude whom no man can number, the vast majority, in the grand total—to the vindication of each several attribute in God; to the praise of the *glory* of His grace! So that each perfection in Him may appear in poise and balance—so that the display of one may not be the adumbration of another—so that He may not seem to hang mid-heaven, obscured, half-hidden, half-eclipsed, the segment of a mutilated sun, but bursting through the clouds, and throwing them behind His back into remoter and remoter horizons, He may shine forth

"A God all o'er consummate, absolute,
Full orbed, in His whole round of rays complete."

In order to this there must be a *choice*. Election is the Alpha of grace—the first, most humbling, and yet most encouraging manifestation of God.

It is the *first manifestation,* since if we cannot stir, God must.

It is a *humbling* manifestation, since it grasps the golden mace of the Divine Sovereignty, swings it aloft, and brains a man of all his thoughts, imaginations, feelings, efforts—lays him prostrate in the dust, and then stoops down and, writing death upon his members, thus destroys that *faith in self which* hinders him from resting upon that which is outside of self, the work of Christ for sinners.

Election is an *encouraging* doctrine, since it as a drag-net cast into the water not to drive away fish but to draw them. If I am the lost creature that the Bible says I am, then since I can never choose to set my affections on God, God must choose to set His affections on me. He must come out and down to me in free and overflowing love. He must begin to work upon me. He must create within me the desires of my heart. He must awaken within me a Divine curiosity. He must make me feel my great necessity, and draw me on to Christ. He must overcome my hesitations, and allay my apprehensions, and dissipate my fears, and bring me to assured, unchangeable repose upon His faithful promise.

Now what is all this but the expansion of the Bible statement, "According as He hath chosen us in Him before the foundation of the world, that we might be holy, not *because* we are holy, but that we *might be* holy and without blame before Him. In love having predestinated us into the adoption of children by Jesus Christ to Himself."

And in all this there is solid comfort and encouragement for every disquieted soul. For since Divine election is impartial—since it finds in the best of us nothing to attract, and in the basest of us nothing to repel—since it comes to give us everything and to exclude us from nothing; why then the worst of sinners, and the worst sinners of the worst, are quite as likely to be swept within the circle of its mighty and compassionate and conquering consolations, as are those who, in the pretentions of an unimpeachable

THE DOCTRINES OF GRACE 159

morality, and who, in the kindly judgments of men, stand nearest of all.

2d. The second element in grace is *absolute redemption*—that Christ dies for the elect part of fallen sinners and for that part alone.

This appears—

1. From what has already been said. The salvation brought in through the reconciliation of the Divine attributes contemplates a part and a part only.

2. It appears from the consistency of the Holy Trinity with itself. If the Father elects, the Son, in perfect sympathy with the Father, cannot enlarge upon that election.

3. It appears from the tenor of the Eternal Covenant— "I have made a covenant with my chosen, I have sworn unto the Beloved my servant, Thy *seed* will I establish forever." Here the covenant is in so many words confined to the seed.

4. It appears from the absurdity of the opposite. For if Christ died for all alike, then He did no more for those who are saved than for those who perish. And if He died for all alike, then He bore the curse for many who are now bearing the curse for themselves, and He suffered punishment for many who are yet lifting up their own eyes in hell, being in torments, and He paid the redemption price for many who are yet paying in their own eternal anguish the wages of sin, which is death. To say this is of course to convict God of the grossest injustice, for it is to represent Him as receiving from the hands of Christ full atonement, and then as dashing down to perdition millions of those for whom Christ had died to atone. The story is told of Pizarro that when he had imprisoned the Peruvian Inca, that monarch, lifting his hand to the level of his head upon the wall behind him, promised to fill the apartment with silver and gold to that level, provided Pizarro would let him go free. Pizarro agreed to this, and then when the loyal subjects of the Inca, by denying themselves to the utmost, had brought together the requisite ransom, Pizarro led forth their beloved Inca, and before their smiling expectant faces put him to excruciating death. *That* Pizarro, lifted and broadened to infinite proportions, is the shadow which a universal atonement projects upon

God—it makes an infinite Pizarro and subverts the very substratum upon which is built His throne.

5. That Christ died for His people alone appears from the fact that otherwise there is no real and complete atonement. By atonement we understand the *work of a substitute*. Now, if Christ was the substitute of all men, He failed, for all men are not saved by Him. But if He was the substitute of His people He did not fail, for His people are saved by Him, and we have an atonement which truly atones, a redemption which truly redeems.

6. The doctrine of universality—shall I say the doctrine of a vague atonement—surrenders certainty while seeking to captivate. Suppose we preach broadly that Christ died for all men and for all alike. The first effect of this preaching, no doubt, will be to brighten men's hopes, to open wide horizons and apparently to bring salvation home to them. But what is the after result? Will not every man, in reflecting, say to himself, "What is this salvation which has been brought home to me? Is it not a benefit common to me with souls already lost? Was it not once theirs as now it is mine? What assurance then can it give me that I, like them, may not be lost? If multitudes have perished for whom Christ has died, why may not I?" In order to certainty then, some other proposition must be brought in—some special, call it narrow interest, if you please, in Christ's death—but something which shall make salvation a fixture and secure upon granitic foundations, that come what may, amid all changes, though mountains be upheaved and hills depart, nothing shall occur to alienate God's loving kindness.

7. Christ died for His people *in such a way* as to save them, or else He is not the faithful Saviour whom we have known and loved and honored. For my part I would rather, infinitely rather, believe that Christ had never redeemed a single soul than believe that He so cast shame, dishonor and reproach upon His own depthless agonies, and upon the very need of an Atonement, as to lose sight of that soul after having gone through what he did to redeem it. Rather, infinitely rather, would I believe that Christ never loved at all than that having loved unto death He

had not strength to love all the way through, but failing in the extreme crisis lost what He died for.

3d. The third element in grace is *quickening*. Is there any such thing as quickening? What does that mean? It means giving life. Can lost man give life to himself? Can nature rise above nature? There is needed, therefore, in addition to the work of the Father, and to the work of the Son, the work of the Spirit. That which is spiritual must be born of the spirit.

When we look around us we see four kinds of life—mineral, vegetable, animal, intellectual. These four kinds of life are different. Can they have anything in common? Can they replace one another? Can the rock by volition turn itself into a tree, the tree transmute itself into an ox, the ox make itself into a man? There are those who say they think so. There are those who have brought in what they are pleased to call *"Development,"* expressly to deny, in face of all the facts, that greatest fact of all, "Ye must be born again!" But that which is not and which cannot be in the least, how shall it be in the greatest? That which is not and cannot be in the seen, how shall it be in the unseen? That which is not and cannot be in the temporal, how shall it be in the eternal? As well might Satan will himself into a seraph as fallen man, by efforts of volition, will himself into that new creation which is called a "child of God."

The Doctrine of Grace then, is this—that dead nature lies on a dead level. That on this dead level God comes in—that the *Father* elects, the *Son*, redeems, the *Spirit* quickens—and that by resurrection lifted to another level, the new life runs on and on and on forever!

The Doctrine of Grace therefore is nothing but the Doctrine of the Holy and Undivided Trinity. It is nothing but saying, "Glory be to the Father, and to the Son, and to the Holy Ghost!" It is nothing but beginning here below the prelude of that new, unspeakable and everlasting song, Holy! Holy! Holy! Lord God Almighty.

II. *How* has this Doctrine of Grace, which bringeth salvation, appeared unto all men? It has appeared unto all men in the *preaching of the Gospel*, which is not distinctively the setting forth of Divine Sovereignty, nor of a new and supernatural birth, but is the offer of Jesus Christ to all men, everywhere, of every condition, irrespective of whatever else be true or untrue—certain or uncertain, clear or dark.

In the Gospel proper there are "neither claims, nor commands, nor duties, nor threatenings." It brings salvation, it does not exact nor demand it. In it there is reported a peace purchased for poor sinners by the blood of Jesus, sufficient in its nature for all—suited to all and free to all who will take it. The Gospel which we get from this book and which we preach is this—For all His people, Jesus Christ stands substitute. They are His people who put their trust in Him. If you trust Him, my brother—if the Spirit draws you, and, what man dare say the Spirit does not draw him? If you *consent*, for consent is everything in religion, you are saved. And how are you saved? Why so saved that if the solid world were split asunder and the graves rent open and the universe itself convulsed —so long as God's throne stands unshaken, and so long as truth is truth and righteousness is righteousness, you are the heir of an eternal life, the crowned possessor of an everlasting glory.

The doctrine of grace *brings* salvation. It tells us that since we can do nothing—nothing whatever, God has done all. That He has gone into the question of our sin and our necessity and sifted it to the bottom—that He has planned largely and effectively for the relief of sinners and the redress of law—that He has righted Himself with Himself—that He has satisfied the claims of justice—that He has satisfied the claims of moral government—that He has satisfied the claims of human conscience, and that He has so settled all things on a new, impregnable, immovable foundation by the Blood of Christ, the smitten Rock of Ages, that those who trust on that foundation cannot be confounded.

My unconverted brother, the Gospel is of such a nature that when it says, "The Blood of Jesus Christ, His Son, cleanseth us from all sin," if you consent to that cleansing you are cleansed. The Gospel is of such a nature that when it says, "He brought in everlasting righteousness," if you consent to that righteousness you are righteous. It

THE DOCTRINES OF GRACE

is of such a nature that when it says, "He hath made Him to be sin for us," if you consent to that *exchange,* to that *transfer,* Christ becomes your *substitute,* He is put into your place, and you are put into His place at once—on the spot.

The one point in religion, then, is *consent.* Toward that point God's Providence, God's Word, God's Spirit—all the forces of His moral empire—urge, incite, and draw men. From that point if men recalcitrate—if they say "I won't," they are lost. *At* that point if men consider—if they give God credit for speaking the truth—if they do Him the honor of venturing on his provision—if they believe in the Lord Jesus Christ—in one word, if they CONSENT, they are saved.

The one question of our moral destiny is the reception or the non-reception, of the Blood atonement!

Such is the Doctrine of Grace. Such is its presentation. Now,

III., and lastly, What is its *practical effect?*

Some say it is too *simple.* It cannot save because there is not enough to it—a man has nothing to do but believe.

Our reply to this is—that simplicity is the ornament of all nobility, and the special grandeur of God. The Gospel is simple, just as Niagara is simple, but capable of bearing on its heaving and mysterious tides each tiny drop that leaps and sparkles there, out, out into the wide Ontario of God's grace, and out again into the measureless Atlantic of His glory. The Gospel is simple only because God behind it does that which is hard and leaves to man that which is easy. The Gospel is simple only because it is free from circumlocution, from mystification, and from what we stigmatize in worldly affairs as "red tape."

> "Oh how unlike the complex works of man
> Heaven's easy, artless, unincumbered plan!
> From *ostentation,* as from weakness, free,
> It stands like the cerulean arch we see,
> Majestic in its own simplicity;
> While, writ upon its portal, from afar
> Conspicuous as the brightness of a star,
> Legible only by the light they give,
> Stand the soul-quickening words—
> *Believe and Live!"*

But it is said that this doctrine of grace *destroys good works*—that it pulls down all we have built up, and makes it of no avail that we have prayed and wept and labored.

Our reply to this is to confirm it—to admit that the Gospel razes Shinar's Tower of brick and slime to its foundation—that it opens a great gulf beneath our feet, into which it flings all our doings and all our experiences and all our deservings, while it cries over their universal demolition "Babylon the Great is *fallen!* is *fallen!* is *fallen!*" We preach as the special and distinctive glory of the Gospel the obliteration of good works as, in any way, in any sense, essential, confirmatory, supplementary, the ground-work of our standing before God. *We affirm with boldness that our good works cannot strengthen our salvation nor our bad works weaken it*—that not in one whit does our salvation depend upon what we commit or omit —upon what we do or fail to do, but only upon this—the reception of Christ.

> "Of all that wisdom teaches this the drift,
> That man is dead in sin, and life's a gift."

But some say the Doctrine of Grace leads to *unholiness*. No! there we stop—*that* we deny!

The Doctrine of Grace is not *built* on good works, because it *creates* them. A man without the indwelling Holy Ghost is dead, but where the Holy Ghost comes and makes him alive, he *is* alive. How? By the Holy Ghost. In what direction? Alive unto God. For the grace of God hath appeared unto all men, teaching us that denying ungodliness and worldly lusts, we should live soberly, righteously and godly in this present world.

The Doctrine of Grace cannot make men unholy—for

1. It has for its *object,* straight through, the glory of God—but unholiness does not glorify Him.

2. The Doctrine of Grace has for its object to magnify the law and to teach us to magnify it—but unholiness does not magnify the law.

3. The Doctrine of Grace has for its object to make us new creatures; but if we are *new* creatures we are different from what we were before—if therefore we were before unholy, now we become holy.

THE DOCTRINES OF GRACE

4. The Doctrine of Grace teaches us to do all things by God's Spirit, but God's Spirit is a holy Spirit; what we do therefore must be holy.

5. The Doctrine of Grace suspends everything on faith, but faith works by love and purifies the heart, and we are sanctified by faith which is in Christ Jesus.

6. The Doctrine of Grace brings us to a perfect rest in God, but then it is a *Sabbath* rest—the eternal Sabbath begun—in which there shall be nothing unholy.

7. The Doctrine of Grace gives us Christ, not only as our Priest to sacrifice for us, but our Prophet to teach us and our King to rule us. We must therefore "beware of Him and obey His voice, for God's name is in Him."

8. The Doctrine of Grace bestows everything, and therefore awakens our gratitude. "We thus judge that if one died for all, then all died, and that He died for all that we who live should not henceforth live unto themselves but unto Him who died for them and rose again."

9. The Doctrine of Grace, so far from abolishing God's law, re-enacts it. It gathers up the Tables broken on Sinai in order to re-cement them and preserve them in the true and living Ark, Christ Jesus, who Himself also has left us an example that we should follow His steps. Upon no men —upon no dispensation have the Ten Commandments been so binding as they are upon us Christians in this dispensation of grace.

10. The Doctrine of Grace is not only a *precept*, it is a *power*. "Our Gospel came unto you," says the Apostle, "not in word only, but in power and in the Holy Ghost. The Holy Ghost is the author of all that is in the saved man. Whatever is not of the Holy Ghost is not of the *New "I,"*—it must therefore be *cast out, crucified, reckoned dead.*

On the other hand—when we say the Holy Ghost is in us—what does that mean? It means that God is in us— working through us—working on and out.

A strawberry runner is shot from the parent stem, for what purpose? That it may take root, become a new plant and bring forth fruit. In like manner I am shot forth out of God, by the infusion of a divine nature, that I in turn rooted and grounded in Christ, may bring forth fruit unto God.

If any man say otherwise—if he say, "Let us therefore continue in sin that grace may abound"—our reply is that of the Apostle—echoed by the consenting voices of redeemed man in all ages—"whose damnation is just!"

Now, unto God the Father, God the Son and God the Holy Ghost be glory evermore. Amen.

THE DOCTRINE OF ELECTION TRUE

Acts xiii:48

"As many as were ordained to eternal life, believed."

The reason why any one believes in Election is, that he finds it in the Bible. No man could ever imagine such a doctrine—for it is, in itself, contrary to the thinkings and the wishes of the human heart. Every one, at first, opposes the doctrine, and it is only after many struggles, under the working of the Spirit of God, that we are made to receive it. A perfect acquiescence in this doctrine—an absolute lying still, in adoring wonder, at the footstool of God's sovereignty, is the last attainment of the sanctified soul in this life—as it is the beginning of heaven.

The reason why any one believes in Election is just this, and *only* this—that God has made it known. Had the Bible been a counterfeit it never could have contained the Doctrine of Election, for men are too averse to such a thought to give it expression much more to give it prominence.

The Bible not only teaches the doctrine, but makes it prominent—so prominent that you can only get rid of Election by getting rid of the Bible. It is the Bible part that is the great difficulty. It is not what believers say, nor what a sound philosophy teaches, but it is what the Scriptures say, that confronts us. No propositions ever laid down by the pulpit are so difficult to receive as is the inspired language itself. This will explain the great dislike of certain passages of Scripture which allude to this topic. Men pass them by— they turn from them—they are angry if they hear them quoted even without a comment. They do their best to twist them from their plain sense—to explain away their meaning and *yet,* after all their explanations, they do not like to hear them or to read them. They feel that their one-sided and disingenuous dealings cannot bear the light of God.

The Bible makes Election prominent. It puts Election *basal* to the entire scheme of grace. It makes it the Supreme law—the underlying principle of the Gospel—that, in harmony with which, all things else have their being and that which if it should fail, the universe would be a ruin.

If this be so—if the Doctrine of Election is in the Bible, then we shall have, either to give up the Bible, or receive the Doctrine.

If the Doctrine *is* in the Bible, then, since we *do not* intend to give up the Bible, we *must* receive it.

Election means choice and "to elect" means to choose, and the Doctrine of Election is the absolute choice of those who are to be saved, from eternity.

Bear with me then I pray you while we consider.

I. The Doctrine of Election as it runs through the Bible.
II. The Doctrine in this particular text.
III. The Doctrine as held by the Church.
IV. The Meaning of the Doctrine.
V. Its practical Value, and

I. The Doctrine of Election as it runs through the Bible.

I prefer to begin with a whole volley of texts,—i. e., to avalanche you with an irresistible pressure of testimonies of the Holy Spirit, and, afterward, to close to a more logical and special presentation of my theme.

If then we turn to the Old Testament we shall read in Deut. 7:7, "The Lord thy God hath chosen thee to be a special people unto Himself. The Lord did not set His love upon you, nor choose you because ye were more in number than any people, for ye were the fewest of all people, but because the Lord loved you." In Neh. 9:7 we go back of this, "Thou art the Lord, the God, who didst choose Abram and gavest him the name Abraham." In I Chron. 28:4, we have David—"The Lord God of Israel chose me." In I Chron. 29:1, he says, "Solomon my son whom God hath chosen." In the Psalms he enlarges on this—"He chose David also His servant." "I have made a covenant with My chosen." "Ye children of Jacob His chosen." "Aaron whom He had chosen." "He brought forth His chosen." "That I may see the good of Thy chosen." Pass from the Psalms to Isaiah and we read—"Thou Israel art my servant, Jacob whom I have chosen. I have chosen thee and not cast thee away." "Ye are my witnesses and my servant whom I have chosen." "I have refined thee but not with silver; I have chosen thee in the furnace of affliction." "Behold My elect in whom My soul delighteth." "Mine elect shall long enjoy the work of their hands."

From the Old Testament let us pass to the Epistles of the New Testament, where we shall expect to find a more direct teaching. Take Romans, "Whom He did predestinate them He also called." "Who shall lay anything to the charge of God's elect." "The children being not yet born neither having done any good or evil—that the purpose of God according to election might stand, it was said to her, the elder shall serve the younger." "For He saith to Moses, I will have mercy on whom I will have mercy—so then it is not of him that willeth nor of him that runneth but of God that showeth mercy." "There remaineth therefore a remnant according to the election of grace." "The election hath obtained it and the rest were blinded."

I Corinthians: "God hath chosen the foolish things of the world and God hath chosen the weak things of the world, and base things of the world and things which are despised hath God chosen, yea and the things that are not, to bring to nought the things that are."

Ephesians: "According as He hath chosen us in Him before the foundation of the world—having predestinated us into the adoption of children by Jesus Christ, in whom we also have obtained an inheritance being predestinated according to the purpose of Him who worketh all things after the counsel of His own will."

Philippians: "To you it is given on the behalf of Christ to believe." "Whose names are written in the Book of Life."

Colossians: "Put on as the elect of God, bowels of mercies."

I Thess.: "God hath not appointed us to wrath but to obtain salvation."

II Thess.: "God hath from the beginning chosen you to salvation through sanctification of the Spirit and belief of the truth."

Timothy: "Who hath saved us and called us with an holy calling, not according to our works but according to His own purpose and grace which was given us in Christ Jesus before the world began."

Titus: "According to the faith of God's *elect*."

James: "Of His own will begat He us."

I Peter: "Elect according to the foreknowledge of God." "The Church elected together with you saluteth you."

John: "The elder unto the elect lady. The children of thine elect sister greet thee."

Jude: "Ungodly men who were before of old ordained to this condemnation."

Revelation: "None shall enter but they which are written in the Lamb's Book of life—in the Book of the life of the Lamb slain from the foundation of the world."

I have reserved however as the strongest class of texts the words of our Lord Jesus Christ in the Gospels.

"I speak not of you all, I know whom I have chosen." "Ye have not chosen Me but I have chosen you." "I have chosen you out of the world." "Many are called but few are chosen." "All that the Father giveth Me shall come to Me." "No man can come to Me except the Father which hath sent Me draw Him." "As thou hast given Him power over all flesh that He might give Eternal life to as many as Thou hast given Him." "Those that Thou gavest Me I have kept." "I pray for them—I pray not for the world but for them which Thou hast given Me." "I thank Thee Oh Father—Lord of heaven and Earth—that Thou hast hid these things from the wise and prudent and hast revealed them unto babes. Even so, Father, for so it seemed good in Thy sight."

From the general survey and scope of the Scriptures as gleaned from assertions of which these are specimens, we come now,

II. To the Doctrine of Election as taught in the text. "As many as were ordained to eternal life believed." These words occur in the Book of the Acts of the Apostles—the only part of the Scripture from which I have not quoted—and they are as strong and full a statement of the doctrine as one could possibly require.

"But do the words behind these teach the doctrine of

THE DOCTRINES OF GRACE

Election?—Do the Greek words teach it?" They most certainly do. Nothing could be more shallow or puerile than the evasions which have been resorted to to disprove this. 300 years ago, the most learned and pious men of the Reformation translated the Greek as they found it, and—for 300 years, against all criticism, this translation stands—even in the Revised New Testament, it stands.

The Arminians and liberals insist that the Greek word means "disposed"—as many as *felt* disposed to have eternal life believed. Of course they believed if they felt disposed to believe. There is nothing very instructive in that—the question is "who disposed them?"

The Greek word is passive—they *were* disposed—i. e. Some one disposed them. I studied Greek six years and then taught it three, in one of our first Seminaries, and have been keeping up with the language ever since, and I simply know that the word τεταγμένοι involves an Outside Agent, in the arrangement. They did not dispose themselves—they *were* disposed—in other words: God did it—i. e., He ordained them.

Dr. Alexander, of Princeton, says: "The violent attempts which have been made to eliminate the doctrine of election, or predestination from this verse, by rendering the verb, *"disposed,"* or, by violent constructions such as that of Socinus—"as many as believed, were ordained," can never change the simple fact that wherever the word occurs elsewhere in the New Testament, it invariably expresses the action of an outside person upon the subject."

"The word τεταγμένοι" says Calvin, "means chosen by the free adoption of God. The mass refused but there was an election. Luke does not say they were ordained to faith, but 'unto life,' and that shows that faith depends on God's election. For, if two hear the doctrine together, and *one* is willing to be taught, while the *other* continues obstinate, *this* is not because the two differ *by nature* but because God makes them to differ, softening the mind and heart of the one by His will."

Spurgeon says: "Attempts have been made to prove that these words do not teach predestination, but these attempts so clearly do violence to language that I shall not waste time in answering them. I read: 'As many as were ordained to eternal life believed' and I shall not twist the text but shall glorify the grace of God by ascribing to that grace the faith of every man. Is it not God who gives the disposition to believe? If men are disposed to have eternal life, does not He—in every case—dispose them? Is it wrong for God to give grace? If it be right for Him to give it—is it wrong for Him to purpose to give it? Would you have Him give it by accident? If it is right for Him to purpose to give grace to-day, it was right for Him to purpose it before to-day—and, since He changes not—from eternity."

But now see,

III. With this Doctrine of the text agree all the Evangelical Confessions in the world. Take for instance the oldest of them—the Waldensian Confession:

"God saves from corruption and damnation those whom He has chosen from the foundations of the world, not for any disposition, faith or holiness He foresaw in them, but of His mere mercy in Christ Jesus, His Son, passing by all the rest according to the irreprehensible reason of His own free will and justice."

Take the Third Article of the Baptist Confession: "By the decree of God, for the manifestation of His glory some men and angels are predestinated or preordained to eternal life through Jesus Christ, to the praise of His glorious grace; others being left to act in their sin to their just condemnation."

Take the 17th Article of the Church of England—the Protestant Episcopal Church. "Predestination to life is the everlasting purpose of God whereby (before the foundations of the world were laid) He hath continually decreed by His counsel, secret to us, to deliver from curse and damnation, those whom He hath chosen in Christ, out of mankind, and to bring them, by Christ to everlasting salvation, as vessels made to honor."

The Westminster or Presbyterian Confession says: "By the decree of God for the manifestation of His glory, some men and angels are predestinated to everlasting life—the number of these is unchangeable."

Our own Reformed Church puts it in this way: "We believe that all the posterity of Adam, being fallen into perdition and ruin by the sin of our first parents, God, then, did manifest Himself such as He is—that is to say, *MERCIFUL* and *JUST*,—*Merciful* since He delivers and preserves from this perdition all whom He, of mere goodness, hath elected in Christ Jesus, our Lord, without respect to their works,—*Just* in leaving others in the fall and perdition wherein they have involved themselves."

Thus—from the Scope of the Scriptures—from the Teaching of the Text and from the Confessions of the Evangelical Church throughout the world, the Doctrine has been established:—that brings us

IV. To the *Meaning* of the doctrine which, in the very treatment of the subject, so far, has been largely forestalled, and

1. It means that God's choice is *absolute*,—that it is a gratuitous election and that it depends on nothing outside of God Himself. He chose because He chose to choose—from no merit or attraction in the creature and from no *foreseen* merit or attraction to *be* in the creature, but simply out of the spontaneous goodness of His own volition which, from the mass of mankind—all equally guilty and all equally deserving of death, selected some—a multitude whom no man can number, to live.

Justice demanded that all should die, but justice cannot demand that, if some shall be saved, *all* must be. That is for God to decide. It rests with Him to save *all*, or *none*, or *few*. Those not elected are simply left to themselves and to their sins, and to the just consequences of their sins.

But some reply: "God chooses people because they are good—because of sundry works which they have done." Who then is good? "There is none that doeth good, no not one,"—and what works are they on the account of which God is obliged to choose men? Not the works of the law, for, "by the deeds of the law shall no flesh be justified." If men cannot be justified by the works of the law, they cannot be elected by them. Besides the Scripture shuts off the cavil by saying: "Not by works of righteousness which we have done but according to His mercy He saved us"—"Not according to our works but according to His own purpose and grace which was given us in Christ Jesus before the world began." If it was *given us*, we did not earn it nor can we.

"But," says another, "God elects men on the foresight of their faith." But God gives faith, therefore He could not have elected men on the ground of any faith which he foresaw. If, among a score of beggars, I determine to give one of them a dime, who will say that I determined to give it, because I foresaw he would have the dime anyhow? What nonsense. The gift of the dime is free—the choice is free, and so faith, the gift of God, is the *result* not the ground of election.

Besides: To say that God elected those whom He foresaw would believe is to deny election. God elected those He foresaw would believe and who were they? None,—absolutely none. *He foresaw that none would believe, not one.* Did He? Then because He foresaw this He had to *elect*, otherwise not one would have believed at all.

2. The Doctrine means that God's choice is *unchangeable.* It is not founded on anything else. It is before everything else. It is before His foreknowledge. He does not decree because He foreknows, but He foreknows because He has fixed it. If not He only guesses. If He foreknows it, He does not guess—it is certain. But if certain, then it is fixed —then He fixed it.

3. Election is *eternal.* "God hath, from the beginning, chosen you." Can any man say, when was that beginning? "In the beginning was the Word,"—from the beginning God hath chosen. Then, if His choice has been from eternity, it will last to eternity. There is the unassailable comfort of the people of God. Nothing can survive to eternity but what came from eternity, and what *has* so come, will. "I have loved thee with an everlasting love, therefore with loving kindness, have I drawn thee—I will never leave thee nor forsake."

4. The Doctrine of Election is *personal.* Here again we meet the evasion that the election is of *Nations*—as Israel— and not of men. But how miserable the shift is will appear when we remember that nations are made up of men—that they are but a collection of *units.* If God chose the Jews, then He chose this Jew and that Jew—as Abram and Moses and David, and what is this but personal election?

Besides: if it were not just to choose a person and rule in favor of that person, rather than another, how can it be just to choose a nation and rule in favor of that nation, and set it up to the exclusion of all other nations? On such a line of special pleading, the choice of a whole nation, being the more tremendous choice becomes the more tremendous crime. Election then is *personal,* God hath chosen *us* in Christ—*"Us"* means believers and believers singly—"He calleth His own sheep by name." Each name is written on the breast plate of the Great High Priest our Surety and our Substitute and therefore may we say and sing:

> "Sons we are by God's Election,
>   Who on Jesus Christ believe,
> By eternal destination,
>   Sovereign grace we now receive,
>   Lord Thy mercy,
> Doth both grace and glory give!"

5. Election is a choice to *holiness.* "God hath from the beginning chosen you unto sanctification of the Spirit and belief of the truth."

The man who says he is elected, and leads a life of sin is a self-contradiction. God chooses the unholy, but they do not remain unholy. He justifies the ungodly, but they do not remain ungodly.

"And belief of the truth." One mark of our election is our willingness to submit our reason to the statements of the Word of God. It is not our Christian consciousness which must guide us. Christian consciousness must be lifted to the plane of scripture. That "Thus saith the Lord" rules with us, is an evidence of our election. There are only two religions in the world—one built on election and the other on free-will. If I adopt the one religion, I break down and submit to God and to the Bible. If not, I erect my Christian consciousness—that is the modern phrase,—"my Christian consciousness" against them and it will betray me.

We come now

V.—To the *Value* of the Doctrine,—of what use is it in a practical way? If I am elected to salvation irrespective of works then I am elected on some other ground—then I am shut up to Christ only.

If I have had some hand in making myself a Christian, I shall always be looking at the progress I make. I shall.

always, more or less, be resting on this or that evidence,—on this, or that thing or hoped for thing, in me or about me. But, when I thoroughly grasp the doctrine of election—I see that I am saved only as a sinner, for the sake of the merits of Christ,—I see that a *naked* faith saves me—a faith irrespective of works although it produces them. How often do we lean upon something else besides Christ—on some other might or strength than that which is from on high. All this is taken away when we believe in election. We are shut up to God and faith only.

Another use of election is that it, as nothing else, humbles us. The other doctrine—that of free-will makes us self-conscious, exclusive, self-righteous, and proud. We become Pharisees. We make ourselves to differ. We look down on others who are less strict and punctilious. "God, I thank thee that I am not as other men are, or even as this Publican" becomes our litany.

But, when we are thoroughly broken—when we see we are sinners, and—at our best, nothing but sinners,—when we realize that we belong to a fallen race—ourselves as weak before temptation and as liable to fall as any, and that it is God alone who makes us to differ, *then* we grow humble and become more pitiful and more compassionate, and our prayer is—"God be merciful to me a sinner."

But then again: the Doctrine of Election is *ennobling*. It makes heroic men. Even the men who, at the present, are most frantic for a change in the creed are proud of the fathers who made it and held it. What men they were—"of whom the world was not worthy." And what *made* them such men? What transformed them from common to uncommon clay? What but the infusion of a Blood-royal? Their principles—their religion, the marrow and the soul of which was the electing love of God.

There is a nobility about the Calvinist which attaches to no other man. His doctrine may seem stern in some aspects —stern as Moses, Elijah and Paul—but it alone can make such men. Arminianism never yet produced a martyr. No man ever yet died for the sake of free-will. In front of the fire he falls from grace, to resume it again when the fire is extinguished. As it was said of one of the leaders in the General Assembly the other day. "He was an iron-clad

Presbyterian at the beginning of the week but at the end he was no longer a son of thunder." Had he been thorough, he would have been the same at the end of the week that he was at the beginning.

Few men, when popular sentiment has lifted it, can dare to stand the storm. Their principles give way because they are not deep enough—genuine. They talk but when the crisis comes, they are lacking. The believer in the good old Doctrine of Predestination has back-bone. You cannot swerve him, though you grind him to powder.

This is the doctrine which has made nations great and men and civilizations splendid. It is the doctrine which in every age—has communicated the highest upward impulse to human life, affairs, and aspiration.

I am led to speak the more boldly, this morning, because of the religious change which is coming over this nation and over our age.

Presbyterian means Predestination. The whole world knows that. And the whole world knows that there is no ground for the simple service and the simple government of the Church to which we belong, save the ground of election, which makes our creed differ, and gives us our theology and life. The reason for our existence is the doctrine which I have defended to-day. To relinquish that doctrine is to drift in one of two directions—toward *ritualism* on the one side or *rationalism* on the other.

The last week has witnessed a movement on the part of a great denomination which is ominous for the future. The new creed, or, as it is called—"A Statement of the Reformed Faith"*—which has been adopted in New York, is a compromise. It is a drawbridge between Calvinism and Arminianism. It can be pulled up with some very strenuous straining, *perhaps,* by the orthodox—but it can be easily let down by the liberals, and it will be. On the whole, it gives the doctrine away.

But let me not close this sermon without a practical appeal to those who have sometimes made this doctrine an objection to their immediate coming to Christ.

To any such I would say: What claim have you, my Brother—a fallen creature—upon any choice of God at all?

*Adopted by the Assembly of 1902.

Do not your sins deserve damnation? Suppose He leaves you, as you are, to be lost, does He do you any injustice? Do you wish to be saved? Then you may be—then you are elected—your very willingness and your wish show that God has been working upon you and working in love. If you long for religion, then God has chosen you to it. If you desire it He has chosen you to it. And, if you do not desire it, and will not have it, and resolutely put the offer of salvation in Christ away from you, why should you blame God if He does not force upon you to have what you do not want, and what you will not have, and what you do not value?

You are not a Universalist. You do not believe that all mankind will be saved, and if *not,* if there be an allotted number, why should you not be of that number? You will be if you do not refuse. You will be if you accept. You will be if you make your calling and election sure, if you say: "I am called, then I will come." "I trust, then I am elected." Both things will be true if you do. Then you will owe salvation to grace—to God's being beforehand with you, and moving on you—as, if not,—if you refuse, you will owe your destruction to your own wilfulness.

You are here in God's house. His Spirit touches you, moves on you now—Believe on the Lord Jesus Christ and be saved.

If you do, you shall see that God's will was first—that *you would never have willed* had not GOD made you willing—that He must have chosen you, for, left to yourself, you never would have chosen Him.

A POPULAR TALK

on

ELECTION AND THE OBJECTIONS

WHICH ARE OFTEN BROUGHT AGAINST IT

The question of Election or *no election* is the question of the Bible on the one side and the human reason on the other.

The moment you begin to speak to men in Christian lands upon the subject of religion that moment carnal reason starts in them and they begin to tell you *what they think* and how it seems to *them.*

Of course, opinions differ. One man believes if he is only moral, and does not drink or swear and is not guilty of any open or secret uncleanness, and if he is decently kind to his neighbors and pays his just debts, that is enough for him. God will receive him when he hands his checks in at the gate.

Another man's opinion is that something more than this is needed. He thinks the Bible ought to come in, and that there ought to be some *doctrine,* as that God is a Trinity and that Christ is God's Son, so that one who denies the Trinity and denies the atonement cannot be saved.

This last man really gives up the whole argument; for if you bring in the Bible at all, you cannot pick and choose. You cannot take Heaven and leave out Hell. You cannot take Christ and believe in the salvation of men without any Christ. You cannot take the New-Birth as a fact and then deny sovereign Election.

If you take the Bible at all, you have got to take it as the Word of God. If it is God's Word, then, when HE speaks that ends it.

If you take the Bible as God's Word, you must expect that Bible to have in it some things that are dark to you. Mystery is dark and God is mysterious. "Lo, these are *parts* of His ways, but how little a portion is heard of Him." (Job xxvi:14.) "How *unsearchable* are His judgments and His ways past finding out!" (Rom. xi:33.) "Great is the *mystery* of godliness." (I. Tim. iii:16.)

If the Bible is the Word of God, it will tell us things that are *strange* to us, things that reason did not know and could not guess. What were the use of God's giving down from Heaven a revelation of things which we already know?

If the Bible is the Word of God, not only will it contain things strange, but *contradictory* to nature. "For My thoughts are not your thoughts; neither are your ways My ways, saith the Lord. Let the wicked forsake his way and the unrighteous man his *thoughts*. For as the heavens are higher than the earth, so are My ways higher than your ways and My thoughts than your thoughts." (Isa. lv:7, 8, 9.) "The natural man receiveth not the things of the Spirit of God neither *can he know them,* but God hath revealed them unto us by His Spirit. (I. Cor. ii:10-14.)

Now Election is one of these things strange and contradictory to nature, which the Bible teaches and which we are bound to receive. A doctrine which we reject at our peril.

I stand here to-night and preach the Word of God. A man steps up to this desk and he says: "This thing, that thing and the other thing which you assert, does not seem true to me."

I answer: *"I do not assert it.* I am not preaching *my* doctrine. What is the good of *my* doctrine, or any other man's doctrine? GOD says it. It is *here in the Book*.

"Well! but," he says: "it does not seem so to me." My reply is: "What difference does it make how it *seems?* If God says it, you've got to square to it."

"But, I can't see it that way!" No more could I once —no more can any man with his natural, blind and unconverted heart. That is just what God says: "The natural man *receiveth not* the things of the Spirit of God, neither *can* he know them because they are spiritually discerned."

You come into God's house then, not to tell God what *you* think; but to find out what HE thinks. That is far more important, because you cannot handle God, and He can handle you.

And who are you, anyhow? A child of yesterday—ignorant, fallible, finite, who have lived your whole life in sin, with now and then a spurt at goodness, from which you fell back.

Who are you, who have read God's Word very little, who have studied it in a comparison of texts, in an honest endeavor to get at its meaning, and its consistency with itself; next to none? Who are you to stand up before your Maker and the Book which one day is to judge you, and say: "I believe *that*," and "I don't believe that *other*." Who are you to contend against God? What is the good of fighting God?

It is at your own peril, you take such an attitude, because this Book is your only Guide-Book to heaven, your only Anchor of hope, your only Title Deed to glory.

Refuse this Book, and you throw away your guide-book through an unknown wilderness, you slip the anchor clenched within the veil, you burn up the title deed of your eternal inheritance.

Cavil with this Book, and you draw the noose around your own neck, you pull the black cap down over your own face, you spring the drop from under you.

The question then is not that of the human reason. "I think this." "I think that." "I think the other." Sir: God is not at your bar, you are at His. Sir: You will be *damned for your thoughts!* "Let the unrighteous forsake them."

It is not what you think; or I think. It is what the Word of God *says*. God has written you a Bible to correct your thoughts; on purpose to teach you better than you *can* think. Dare to reject the Bible, at your peril.

Election is a doctrine which no human reason could have discovered. It is a doctrine against which the human reason universally, at first, and always rebels. It is a doctrine, however, to which the human reason, if ever saved, must consent. "He that is of God, heareth the words of God. He that receiveth not My words, hath one that judgeth him; the word that I have spoken, the same shall judge him in the last day." (Joh. 8:47, 12:48.)

"Oh, but my friends do not think so!" Then you have got to side with God in spite of your friends.

"Oh, but it will be a cross to me, and I don't half understand it!" All right, you have got to take up that cross and follow your light, and cling to your God. "Let God be true, but every man a liar."

I. The Truth of the Doctrine.

Election is in the Bible. From cover to cover it is in the Bible. It is the great doctrine of the Bible; more important —I will explain what I mean by and by—more important, than even the cross.

I cannot now begin with Genesis, and show how God chose Abel and rejected Cain. How "the children not yet being born, neither having done good or evil, that election might not be of works, God loved Jacob, as St. Paul tells us, (Rom. ix:11), and rejected Esau.

I cannot follow down the whole book. Time affords me opportunity for only a few texts, but they are enough. Each one is a bullet, a hot shot, a 64-pound cannon-ball; no resisting, no standing, no evading, no *dodging* it.

"As many as were ordained to eternal life, believed." (Acts 13:48.)

"According as He hath chosen us in Him before the foundation of the world that we should be holy," not because we were holy, nor because He foresaw we would be holy, but that we *should be holy, to make* us holy. "Having predestinated us unto the adoption of children." (Eph. i:4, 5.)

"Many are called, but few are chosen." (Matt. xx:16.)

"God hath from the beginning chosen you unto salvation." (2 Thess. ii:13.)

"I speak not of all, I know whom I have chosen." (John xiii:18.)

"Ye have not chosen me, but I have chosen you." (John xv:16.)

"If ye were of the world, the world would love his own; but because ye are not of the world, but *I have chosen you* out of the world, therefore the world hateth you" (John xv:19).

"What then? Israel hath not obtained that which he seeketh for (though he was a 'seeker,') but the election hath obtained it and the rest were blinded" (Rom. xi:7).

THE DOCTRINES OF GRACE

"Even so then, at the present time, there remaineth a *remnant*, according to the election of grace" (Rom. xi:5), and

"We are bound to give thanks always to God for you, brethren beloved of the Lord, because God hath from the beginning CHOSEN you to salvation THROUGH sanctification of the Spirit and *belief of the truth,* whereunto He called you by our GOSPEL to the obtaining of the glory of our Lord Jesus Christ" (2 Thess. ii:13, 14).

Of course it is perfectly clear that I cannot quote the whole Bible to-night. I have not the time, nor indeed is it needed. A man who is determined to steel himself against God, and reject one single text, will also reject 20,000.

Election is in the Bible, and *Sovereign* Election. "For He saith to Moses, I will have mercy on whom I will have mercy; and I will have compassion on whom I will have compassion. So then it is not of him that willeth, nor of him that runneth, but of God that showeth mercy" (Rom. ix:15, 16).

"Therefore He hath mercy on whom He will have mercy, and whom He will He hardeneth." It does not say: "They harden themselves;" it says: "*He* hardeneth" (Rom. ix:18).

"Nay, but O man, who art thou that repliest against God? Hath not the potter power over the clay, of the same lump to make one vessel unto honor, and another to dishonor?" (Rom. ix:20, 21.)

"To them which stumble at the word, being disobedient whereunto also they were *appointed* (1 Pet. ii:8). "Ungodly men which were before *ordained* to this condemnation." (Jude 4.)

Not only is Election in the Bible, and *Sovereign* Election; but also PRETERITION, or Passing by.

Of course if God chooses some He passes by others. That is as clear as the nose on your face or as sunlight at noon.

God, when He chose Elisha, passed by ten thousand other men just as likely and just as fit for service as he. He chose Elisha first and then He fitted him. It says so. He put him right into training under Elijah. More than this, He gave him a double portion of the spirit. A man is dead until he receives the *double* portion of the spirit. Not common grace alone which all men have, but *double* grace which all men have not. The first sign of Election is the moving, drawing, working and *effectual working* of the Spirit. The Holy Ghost makes us willing in the day of God's power. He makes us believe what once we did not believe and love what once we did not love—"therefore, if any man be in Christ, he is a new creature; old things are passed away; behold! all things are become new" (2 Cor. v:17).

God chooses some and passes by others. I do not want to be passed by, and, if I can help it, I do not mean to be either. I propose, therefore, to bow right down to God's word and let Him do with me as He will. I believe if I do that, He will be gracious. In any case He will do right, for what do I merit from Him but damnation? I am not in a situation to dictate terms to Jehovah.

God passes by, and He is bound to have some of us *see* this, and cry out for mercy.

I am touching on Preterition to-night. Why do I touch it? Because the air is full of it.

Because God has intended to arouse a sleepy Church and He has permitted *enemies* inside the Church, calling themselves *ministers*, to raise this question. We have not raised it. We are satisfied with our Confession. We have been preaching the Gospel along in a sleepy sort of affectionate way, and all at once men begin to *contradict* God and raise discussion and set the Church and world on fire.

Yet God intended it to rouse a sleepy Church and vindicate His sovereign glory.

This week I received a letter from one of our Sunday School teachers, which makes this point so well, that I will give you his letter:

DEAR PASTOR—Have you noticed the Providence in connection with next Sunday's lesson? About three years ago, the International Committee met and picked out the Course of Lessons for 1890, little knowing what would happen in the meantime. For the last three months the world and Church have been agitated over the "Pro" and "Con" in regard to Preterition. *Now*, after all the wise men have had their say, on next Sunday every one (except the Episcopalians), whether for or against—in America, Germany, France, the Sandwich Islands and China must teach Preterition, using Christ's own words and His two examples"—"Many *widows* were in Israel, but to none of them was Elias sent, but to Sarepta to a woman which was a widow"—"Many *lepers* were in Israel in the time of Elisha, but none of them were cleansed save Naaman the Syrian." "I will have mercy on whom I will have mercy, and I will have compassion on whom I will have compassion." "Ye believe not, because ye are not of my sheep."

"You say then, that God made some men to damn them?" No! I don't say so. I deny it. I simply stand by the Bible, and I take and put texts in plain English, and in their plain and straight-forward sense. God can pass by a sinner who, for his sins deserves hell-fire, without being charged with making that sinner to damn him. God made *man,* and man made himself a *sinner,* and man himself must take the consequences of that. Whoever says I say, "God made men to damn them," slanders me. It is a lie!

The Doctrine of the Bible is that fallen sinners—notice now, *fallen* SINNERS deserve nothing from God but damnation. If He damns them, then they get their desert—if He passes by them, I say, and damns them for sin, because they are *sinners,* they get their desert. If He *saves* them, they do not get their desert, they get mercy.

Now, God does not save all men. Some men go to hell, and go there because they deserve it.

That is all that we say. Only, *when* men are saved, it is God who makes the difference, and not the men themselves. It is not of him that *willeth,* let him will never so hard; men are not born again by the will of the flesh. It is *not* of him that willeth. He cannot will. He is too fallen. It is God who shows mercy, who melts down his will and gives him a good will—or, as the Bible puts it—*makes* him willing in the day of His power.

Put in a nut-shell, our doctrine simply is this: *If any man be saved, it is God's will that saves him; if any man be damned, it is his own will damns him.* That is our doctrine, that is all that we teach and believe.

That is the doctrine of the Reformed Church and of all the Calvinists. It is the doctrine of the Westminster Confession. It is the doctrine of the Church of England. [See the 17th of the 39 articles.] It is the doctrine of the Baptists. Take the third article of the Old Baptist Confession: "By the decree of God, for the manifestation of His glory, some men and angels are predestinated, or foreordained to eternal life through Jesus Christ, to the praise of his glorious grace; others being left to act in their sin, to their just condemnation, to the praise of His glorious justice."

That is the doctrine of the Reformed Church sustained by all the holy creeds of Christendom. It is the doctrine of the Waldenses. It is the doctrine of Augustine; the doctrine of Paul; the doctrine of Jesus: "I thank Thee, O Father, Lord of heaven and earth, because Thou hast hid these things from the wise and prudent, and hast revealed them unto babes. Even so, Father, for so it seemed good in Thy sight."

Antiquity backs us. The Bible backs us. If any man be damned, his own sin; his own willfulness damns him. If any man be saved, God's mercy saves him; *God's will saves him.* By that doctrine we stand. That is the doctrine. now

II. What is the good of the doctrine? What is its working, its practical power?

It is a mighty power, so mighty that I do not know that I ever preached it directly without the conversion of souls.

I use it for *business*. I preach Election, myself an elect minister, believing that *some are elected*, and that God will give me those souls. I preach it expecting results—expecting them to-night. I preach it in reliance on God that He will send down His power.

1. Then election shows the *justice of God*. Suppose that God said in His law, "The soul that sinneth it shall die;" and men went on to sin and nobody did die, how could we ever know that God's justice was anything more than a sham? How could we know, if no sinner ever was damned, that there was in God any honest and resolute justice?

"Oh but we should see it in the case of the devils!" I beg your pardon—we never should see it. We should hear of it by the hearing of the ear, that is all. We never believe in anything until it comes *home* to us.

Besides, if God damns devils for sin, why not also damn

THE DOCTRINES OF GRACE

men? Are we any better than they? Is human nature any better than angelic nature?"

If God had saved all sinners—all our race, there would have been a question forever, even in heaven, whether we did not merit it—whether we were not somehow better—less guilty than they?

If God had saved us all; sin, to all eternity, would have been a light thing to us. What makes us see and feel sin is *being found out,* and being found out when we know that we must be punished.

A man never feels sin so long as he is secure. It is the fear of being found out—*i. e.* of being punished, which brings sin's enormity home to him.

Now, when in heaven we shall look down and see men damned and burning for ages for just the things and *only* the things that *we* did, we shall get, to all eternity, a deeper, deeper sense of what sin is; and shall cry with *newer* and profounder accents, "Holy!" "Holy!" "Holy!"

And that brings me to say what I said in the beginning of this address—that if a man is going to deny one of these two things—Election or the Gospel, he had better deny the Gospel than Election.

Why? Why, because Election is more fundamental—lies back of the Gospel. He who denies the Gospel shuts out mercy of course. He claims that men get their deserts, and that this race is ruined universally without any hope—just like the devils. This ruins *man* but does not ruin *God.* The denial of Election ruins God. It denies His Sovereignty. It denies that He may do as He will with His own. It denies His government—His right to punish wicked fallen creatures. It obliges Him to save them—will He, nill He. It makes *their* will, not His will, the governing and overriding principle. They run the universe and not He. It breaks down the exclusive walls of heaven and leaves the godless universe to roll, like a deluge, over God's prostrate sceptre and throne. A God with His hands tied is no God. A God who cannot exercise a sovereign prerogative based upon justice is no God. He is littler—smaller than the Governor of the State of New Jersey, who can pardon or refuse to grant pardon for reasons sufficient to himself. A God without Election were a God without a government

—without a throne—without respectability, or personality. A God *obliterated*—sponged out. Election saves God by showing His justice. He does not spare all when he might, if he would; in order that sin may be seen, and seen—on a scale sufficiently grand to vindicate God—to get its deserts.

2. Election shows the *mercy of God*. Mercy is favor to the undeserving—to the hell-deserving.

Very well. Election lets some go to hell; then we see that we ought all to go there. But mercy steps in like a drag-net and draws out a multitude no man can number.

This multitude is not saved for what it deserves; if it got its deserts it would go down to hell with the rest. All it can say is, "I deserve to be damned, but God has had mercy"—

> "A monument of grace,
>   A sinner saved by blood;
> The streams of love I trace
>   Up to their fountain—God;
> And in His mighty breast I see,
> Eternal thoughts of love to me."

3. Election brings the sinner to a true *submission*. He sees this thing is more serious. It is not simply a flutter and flurry and get men into the church. If men remain without a new birth and saving faith—what Scripture calls the faith of God's elect—you may get them anywhere, everywhere, and they are rebels still. They are aliens and foreigners still. They are ready at any pretense to desert—always ready to criticize and cavil, and argue and quarrel with God.

Now Election shows a man that God is not under *his* government, but that he is under *God's* government. That God is not standing before *his* bar, but he before *God's*.

The question then is not "How he shall handle God," but "How God *may* handle him." If he is not careful, God will pass by him. If he is too noisy, too bold, and too self-confident, God may take away the Holy Ghost and leave him to the unpardonable sin. He is of no account anyhow—a drop in the ocean. His salvation is of far more importance to him than it can be to God.

He had better, then, get down before God and sue humbly for mercy. If I saw a train of cars thundering down, and myself on the track, and that to fall flat between the rails was my only salvation, I would fall flat. I would not stand up and argue with the locomotive that it ought not to run on those tracks, or run so precisely, or so fast, or that it ought to stop. If I saw it coming, I'd DROP.

Sinner what is the use of fighting with God? You carry your point to your own satisfaction, but you are damned all the same. God does not care for your point.

> Sinner art thou still secure,
> Wilt thou still refuse to pray,
> Can thine heart or hand endure.
> In the Lord's avenging day?
> See his mighty arm is bared,
> Awful terrors clothe His brow,
> For His judgments stand prepared,
> Thou must either break or bow.

Down! Down with you! Down in the dust, and cry "If He slay me it would be *just,* yet, though He slay me, still will I trust in Him."

4. Election *kills,* at the root, *salvation by merits* and works. Any movement of the will is a work. It is something from *me,* which *I* do. It may not run out into the grosser forms of Popish penance; it may remain the undeveloped Protestant repentance—that is seeking, resolving, or trying to do, or to trust. Election, by laying the axe at the root of the tree and declaring "it is not of him that *willeth,*" cuts human merit up both root and branch, and plants a system solitary, isolated, separated by a bridgeless chasm from every other system of religion upon earth.

That brings in the last item; and

5. Election makes a sinner see and feel his *dependence upon God's Spirit.*

If ever you are to be saved, my Brother; you will be saved by God's Spirit. Give up every notion of saving yourself; or helping to save your own self and look away from yourself, to Christ, by the help of His Spirit.

"If I am elect, I shall be saved, let me do what I will!"

No, you will not be. If you are elect, you will show the *signs* of election.

One of those signs is to quit playing with conscience and

cavilling and quarreling with Scripture. A man who is elected swallows God's word whole. I would rather chew and swallow this Bible down, leaf after leaf, covers and all, than deny one single word in it.

A man who is elect doesn't joke and palter and play with serious things. He is humble.

A man who is elect reads his Bible. He reads it for light. He reads it and prays as he reads. He reads it on his knees and turns it into prayer, "Open Thou mine eyes that I may behold wondrous things out of Thy Law."

A man who is elect, *prays*. If God has elected you, He is drawing you by His Spirit, and the first thing He draws you to do is to pray; "O God do not pass by me! Do not take Thy Spirit from me. I am bad enough now, what will I be if left by the Spirit?"

A man who is elect is in *earnest*. He doesn't get to church about once in three or four times; or once, say a quarter. He does not put off God. He knows he is a poor fool, and wishes that God would make him wise to salvation. He therefore heeds the monition: "Hear instruction and be wise, and refuse it not. Blessed is the man that heareth, watching *daily* at my gates, waiting at the post of my doors."

A man who is elect follows the Spirit, cherishes the Spirit, yields to the Spirit, is afraid to grieve the Spirit.

He *follows* the Spirit. But the Spirit leads him to Christ, to trust in the Lord Jesus Christ.

If you are elect, my dear friend, you will look for these marks; above all you will ask yourself, "Do I believe upon Christ? Do I risk myself helpless, on Christ? Do I believe God's promise when He says He will save me, if I trust over, just as I am, on the Lord Jesus Christ?"

Do I trust? And do I make that all? Do I rest on the blood, and that ONLY. Do I see more virtue in Christ's Blood to save, than in all the sins of my life and the sin of my nature, to damn me?

Do I rest *now?* Do I trust NOW? Then what? Then I am elect.

You come to Christ, and then you will know—not until then, your election of God. Election is not first, but Christ first.

THE DOCTRINES OF GRACE

You have seen somewhere, perhaps, the story of Malachi, a sturdy Calvinist of Cornwall. An Arminian brother owed him £2. "Malachi," said the brother, "am I predestinated to pay you that debt?" "Put the £2 into my hand," said Malachi, stretching out his broad palm, "and I'll tell you at once." Believe on the Lord Jesus Christ, and then, in the Blood, you will spell your election. Election is an *ex post facto* assurance. Do, and then you will know—obey, and then you are blest; surely a natural common-sense order. If you are trusting in Christ I will tell you how you got to that point. You got there because the Spirit drew you. You may not have been conscious of the drawing; you may not have discerned the supernatural, but it was there. Inch by inch the Spirit drew you—little by little the Spirit made you willing. "I girded thee though thou has not known me," that is the sacred secret of your spiritual life. God sent the Spirit, and because He chose to send the Spirit, and the choice runs back to everlasting; for right well you know that if God had not chosen you, you never would have chosen Him.

If any man is *non-elect* he will not be damned, let him do as he pleases. He will only be damned if *he sins against light*.

If any man is *elect* he will not be saved let him do as he pleases, he will only be saved *as he trusts on the Lord Jesus Christ,* and he will only trust as the Spirit draws him to trust, and I believe the Holy Ghost is drawing some now.